We must, however, acknowledge, as it seems to me, that man with all his noble qualities... still bears in his bodily frame the indelible stamp of his lowly origin.

■ Charles Darwin

Murder in the

West Bottoms

Published by Merit books. Printed in the United States

Publication Date: Nov 11 2009
Page Count: 284
Binding Type: US Trade Paper
Trim Size: 5.25" x 8"
Language: English
Color: Black and White
Related Categories: Drama / General

ISBN: 1449596053
EAN13: 9781449596057

Fourth Street Books | MT | USA

Email: FLBodeen@gmail.com

Web: http://4thstbooks.com

Acknowledgements

I would like to thank my wife, Susan, for her support during the writing of this novel; my daughter, Lyndsey for helping edit the manuscript; my daughter Farrel for her help in marketing and sales; my daughter, Carey, for her legal advice; my son, Ross, for his positive attitude and encouragement; my brother, Don, for reading a very early draft of my manuscript and encouraging me to continue; my good friends Gary B. and A. P. Rossinger for their encouragement; My truck-driving friends, Dan and Sandy, and Mike W. for taking West Bottoms on the road; Proofreader Catherine A. for having the *patience* to read my manuscript.

Thanks to everyone!

Joe

For my mother, Millie

Joseph Drindall

Chapter 1

I had a headache the day I got fired, I remember that... but I was drinking a lot back then, so I pretty much had a headache everyday so maybe it's not so much a memory as an educated guess. Beer was my drink of choice, at least to begin with. I'd drink somewhere between twelve and eighteen a day, sometimes more. I didn't want to get to the point where I was a "case a day" man, but eventually I did. Eventually I would drink more than a case a day. Eventually I'd drink anything with alcohol in it.

I have a difficult time remembering things from back then. I kept getting a paycheck every month, so I must have been working during that time. "Functional alcoholic" I guess they'd call me at an A. A. meeting although I don't think I was functioning worth a shit. I can't remember functioning. I remember looking and feeling like hell most of the time and just sort of going through life on autopilot. All those days and all those memories have just kind of melded into one vague memory of one vague day.

I finally quit drinking... oh I guess about three years ago now; too late to keep the family together. I miss it... drinking that is. I Miss smoking too, but at 47 I just can't take chances with my health like I used to. I tried drinking socially for a while, but it didn't work out too well. When I'd go to a social setting where there would be alcohol, I'd drink rather moderately, at least for a while, that is until I left the party, which was always pretty early so I could go home and drink more. I'd stop on my way home and pick up a twelver and drink all of them before bed. Publicly I was a moderate, social drinker, but behind closed doors, I was a full-blown alcoholic.

I wish I had quit before my wife packed up the kids and left. If she'd given me half a chance to get my shit together, we could have worked it out. It wasn't her fault though. I was a drunk and drunks don't just stop drinking over night. Ah hell. Who am I kidding? She couldn't stand my drunk ass anymore. She put up with a lot from me. She put up with me passing out in my easy chair every night in front of the TV and not going to bed until four or five in the morning, sometimes not at all. I do miss her, though. I really miss the kids.

After she left, I got depressed and really started hitting it heavy. I was drinking a beer or two for breakfast, another around 10:00 am and of course I'd have a few for lunch. Most days, I'd cut out early in the afternoon and head for the nearest bar where I'd drink several before going home. I'd go along that way throughout the day, every day. Then when I'd get home, I'd down another ten or twelve, more if I had it. I kept my beer fridge pretty well stocked. It was a big fridge. I could fit about four cases in it at once, so I only had to restock once a week, usually on Saturdays. Course I had a couple warm cases ready for the fridge in the event that I ran out of cold ones. I thought buying only on the weekends made me look less like a drunk. I'd buy my beer at different stores each week. I figured that way no one would know how much beer I was actually drinking. A drunk will do things like that, and for all I know, it might actually work. If you buy six or seven cases at one place, you can say you're stocking up for a party. Then if you don't purchase beer at the same place for a month or six weeks, how do they know?

On the other hand, people are smarter than we sometimes think. If you drink in public, someone is going to notice you at some point and realize you have a problem. It's just the way it is.

Anyway, it doesn't really matter because I finally got my ass canned for incompetency about two years ago. Man I was a drunk by then. Incompetent? That's the understatement of the decade. I deserved it. I wasn't doing shit the last six months. I was in no shape to meet with clients, hell I couldn't even remember to shave in the mornings... well I remembered, I just didn't give a shit about my appearance. I didn't even give a shit if I found my way home at night. Sometimes I didn't.

Occasionally I'd wake up in my car outside a bar downtown and not know where I was or how I'd gotten there. That happened several times. I remember once waking up in a park across the street from a bar I used to frequent. I'd gone there to puke. I must have passed out. When I woke up in the morning, everything was dark and I was really cold. I lifted my head up and realized it had snowed about six inches during the night. It was like 8:00 in the morning and people were going to work. Here I was a pile of snow with a head sticking out. People were looking at me like "what a loser." I got up, shook the snow off, got in my car and went to work. Course I drank a couple of beers that I found in the backseat on my way.

I think it was along about then I got fired. It might even have been that very day. I don't remember for sure how long I worked after waking up in the park that morning. Then again, it probably didn't help that I got drunk and put the moves on the boss's wife at a Halloween party. It was one of those occasions when classy people dress up like low class hookers, pimps and bums. Everyone was really getting into it, especially the boss's wife, Elaine. God she made a hot-looking hooker, and she was really playing the part too saying things like, "I bet you prefer to be on top." Man, I really thought she wanted me. What an idiot. What a stupid mistake by a drunken idiot.

I remember I had friends once; friends who shared my occupation and who would accompany me to the Blue Palace for drinks after work. We'd discuss the events of the day, the cases, and, although it was forbidden by the firm, the clients. Of course we weren't supposed to discuss these cases with each another. We were supposed to protect the client's identity but none of us ever did. Oh we never mentioned any names, but we didn't have to. Everyone knew what cases were being handled by whom. Lawyers talk amongst themselves. So do cops, doctors, and college professors. Don't ever let anyone tell you different. We're all human, and humans talk.

So I was fired from the best law firm in Kansas City, Higgins, Rawlins, and Jones, attorneys at law. I was part of a great team for twenty years. On my way up the corporate ladder, I was next in line for a partnership: Higgins, Rawlins, Jones, and Chandler, Attorneys at law. Royal Sage Chandler, partner in the biggest law firm in town. Nope. Wasn't meant to be. Booze and that damn Elaine and her hot-ass, hooker body would see to that.

So there I was sitting outside the boss's office holding my head in my hands thinking about asking Verna for a couple of aspirin for my headache. Verna was an early thirty-something blond who was the latest in the boss's long list of receptionists. Just then her phone rang. "Yes, Sir," she said.

"Mr. Chandler?" Verna said, looking at me. "Mr. Higgins will see you now."

I stood up and walked toward the solid oak door with the gold plaque that read "Gilbert M. Higgins, Sr. Partner."

"Come on in, Sage," Higgins said in response to my knocking on his big, oak door. I entered, and there he was, sitting behind his huge, oak desk, smiling like a monkey that had just licked a hallucinogenic toad. Gilbert Higgins, head partner of the firm. Early sixty's, still had jet black hair except on his temples and sideburns which were graying giving him what they used to refer to as the "distinguished" look. He glanced around at his fellow executives all assembled around his huge oak meeting table. There they were all dressed to kill in their Armani suits showing no emotion whatsoever in their well-practiced poker-faces, each giving a slight smile as my eyes met his. The bastards bared a striking resemblance to the committee who sat in this very office some twenty years ago during my interview, although some of the faces had changed. Some guys had retired, others had died, but somehow sitting around the big oak table they all looked the same to me.

Higgins got up from behind his big desk and sauntered over to take his place at the head of the table. "Please Sage," he said, gesturing to the open chair at the foot of the table. "Have a seat."

I sat down and looked across the table at Higgins. "You want a drink?" he asked. I couldn't help but notice the disdain in his voice. I thought about it. I almost accepted, but good judgment got the better of me and I declined. God did I want a drink. I wanted a bunch of drinks, but I knew that would be a mistake.

"Well," he said. "We might as well get right to it then."

I nodded once at him. "Might as well," I managed.

"Sage," he began, "this isn't easy for me to say." He paused. "But we've noticed your work hasn't been up to par lately. Actually it hasn't been for quite a long time now." He looked around the table.

"We," he always used the word 'we' even though everyone knows Higgins makes his own rules.

"We are wondering if something could be wrong… Trouble at home maybe, or some kind of personal matter?"

"Well," I began. "No. Things are pretty good."

"Oh? Nothing at all wrong?"

I hesitated. I thought about denying it. Acting as though I had no idea what he was talking about. Then something in me said, "Fuck it." Just tell him the truth. Lying had become a bad habit and my lies were catching up with me. I was sick of trying to remember the lies I'd told and how they tied together. I was just sick, plain and simple.

"It's been tough getting along alone since the wife left," I blurted. No response, only silence. I continued. "I guess I miss her and the kids." A look of surprise came across Higgins face. I couldn't tell if it was genuine or not.

"I was under the impression you had joint custody of your kids," he said. That was true. I *had* joint custody, but since I never picked them up on weekends like I was supposed to, custody was taken away. I never said anything to anyone. I didn't even go to court to try to refute it.

"Yeah… well I guess I… I guess we…" I had nothing. Besides it was none of their damn business anyway and I didn't feel like telling them anything about my personal life. As it happened, I didn't have to.

"So you started drinking pretty heavily, didn't you Sage?" There it was, out on the table. He knew.

"Yeah," I said, "I guess I did"

"The Thompson deal last month. Did we lose that because of your drinking?"

"Well that was part of it, I suppose." I didn't remember what the other part was, but I knew something had happened just before Thompson pulled out of the real estate deal Higgins was talking about. Something I had said to Thompson on the phone, but couldn't remember what it was for certain.

"What else happened, Sage?"

"I'm not sure. I think I may have said something that pissed him off."

"And what was that?"

"It might have been something about his being a greedy prick."

He looked around again at his fellow ax men before returning his gaze to me. Shaking his head he said, "Well Sage, I'm afraid we can't go along this way any longer." There was that "we" again. He didn't mean "'we". He meant "me". Why didn't he just say "You Sage. You are the problem. Get the fuck out of here!"

"So what do you suggest we do?" I asked making a point of using his favorite word. If he noticed, he didn't let on.

"Well we are obligated to send you to rehab, if that's something that you'd be willing to do." I looked around the table at the other men and watched as each one averted his eyes. It made me feel small. I felt way too damn sober to deal with this situation.

"Maybe" I said. "I will have that drink after all."

"You think you should?"

"Hell Gil, I might as well have one last drink with you guys before 'we' flush my career down the shitter forever."

Higgins sauntered over to his liquor cabinet and found what he said was his best brandy. "Is Hennessey OK?" he asked.

"If that's the best you have" I said, "but don't you think given the circumstances that you could... you know, break out the good stuff?"

"Well it's all I have!"

"Well then it'll have to do, won't it?"

I was in no mood for his bullshit. Not that Hennessey is a bad brandy, far from it, but I knew Higgins had the really expensive stuff stored in there somewhere and I figured that after twenty years of service I deserved the best, whatever that was. If Hennessey was the best he had then fine. It could have been E & J as long as that was the best he had in his liquor cabinet, but I knew what he was giving me wasn't the best he had. What a prick. He'd always been a prick. Being a prick is a requirement in corporate law. They should have a prick test as an entry exam for law school. If you don't score at least 85% on the prick test, then you'd better check into Med School.

I wanted to tell Higgins what a prick I thought he was. I had seen him break out a bottle of Ragnaud-Sabourin before, but he couldn't offer me any of that. Oh no. Be a fucker! Fine! I could be a prick too.

"So what is it you want from me, Gilbert?" I asked making a special point of putting the "bert" part on the end of his name. He hated that.

"I was of the opinion we'd already come to an agreement on that." he said.

"No... Not really. What is it you expect of me?"

Higgins brought me my brandy and made a big show of presenting to me. He then turned and reclaimed his seat at the head of his table. I almost felt like he couldn't speak unless he was seated in his "special" place at the table. I wanted to tell him so. I wanted to tell him so many things.

"Well" he began, "If you'd be willing to go to rehab, we could -"

"You know what Gil? Fuck you. Fuck you and your rehab. Fuck you and your brandy. Fuck you and your secretary of the month, and most of all fuck your God Damn, chicken shit law firm."

Higgins looked around at all the people seated at the table like he was actually offended. "I'm certain your father would be very ashamed of you, Mr., Chandler."

"No doubt" I said. "I am ashamed of me too... working for a conniving, swindling, fuck like you for all these years."

"Well" Higgins said. "I've never been so insulted in all my life."

"Good" I said. "Then I hold the record, don't I?"

With that, I stood and walked out the big oak door and left Higgins, Rawlins, and Jones forever. I didn't even touch my brandy, which made me feel good. Fuckers! Calling me an alky when every swinging dick that worked for that law firm was at least as bad as me or worse... Well, on second thought, that's probably not true, but they do drink heavy at times.

So there it was. My career as an attorney was finished forever. Surprisingly, I didn't seem to care that much. I hated being a lawyer. It was driving me crazy. So I left Higgins, Rawlins, and Jones with the few items I had in my desk drawer and not much else. I suppose I should have left my dignity behind too, but I didn't.

Chapter 2

So that's how I got where I am today; working as a private investigator and part time skip chaser. My career as a lawyer was ruined. There was no way any of the local firms were going to hire me after being let go from the biggest law firm in town. Luckily for me, I'd made a good living for 20 years, invested well thanks to a shrewd investment banker, who was also a client. He invested my money in tech companies early on and got out before the big "dot com" crash of the late '90s'. I did very well. Even after losing half of it in the divorce, I still have enough money to live for the rest of my life as long as I don't live beyond my means, which trust me, I don't. Without the cost of home ownership, low rent, and no booze bill, I can easily get by on $35,000 a year, which is almost what the interest on my various saving accounts and mutual funds amounts to. I just needed a little subsidy; a part time job, hence, the private investigator gig.

I really hate Kansas City; although, if I were a musician I could maybe play in a blues band and earn enough extra money to get by, but musician I am not. Moving to a new city is out of the question for me. I'm a native Montanan and have never liked big cities. I just don't fit in. I like the small town where everyone knows everyone and a major crime is when a bunch of kids might break some windows or egg a house on Halloween. Here, there's a murder committed almost every night, at least one robbery or burglary, several cars stolen, various acts of vandalism; it's no place for a country boy.

I grew up in Stevensville, Montana, a little town south of Missoula. I attended school there and was a pretty decent tight end on the Stevensville High School football team. My father was an attorney in Missoula. Back then, I wasn't thinking about my future. None of us were. We were busy hot-rodding our cars so we could drive up to Missoula and cruise the drag on Friday or Saturday nights looking for chicks.

After high school, I attended the University of Montana in Missoula with several of my friends. During my freshman and sophomore years, there was plenty of beer to drink and girls to chase. I had the time of my life.

I took a job with the U.S. Forest Service the summer after my sophomore year and loved it. It made we want to go into the Forestry Program at the University and become a "Timber Beast" but my father wouldn't hear of it. He wanted me to become an attorney. His father had been an attorney, and so had his grandfather. It was a family tradition. "Besides," my father would say. "Foresters don't make any money."

So I completed my undergrad degree and applied to the University's Law School. I've always thought my father must have pulled some strings because I've never really felt like I had the aptitude for law school. I'm really not the sit-behind-the-desk kind of guy. I like working outdoors, especially in the mountains. Somehow I was accepted into law school and I gutted it out and managed to graduate and pass the Montana Bar Exam.

I was offered the job with the Higgins and Rawlins law firm in Kansas City right out of law school. I always figured dad had something to do with that too, but I couldn't prove it.

Anyway, once I got my act together and quit the booze, I was able to talk Kim into letting me see the kids every other weekend again, which is the main reason I can't leave Kansas City. Speaking of quitting the booze, it really wasn't that hard after the first few weeks. Oh I went through all the classic alcoholic withdrawal symptoms from night sweats to bad, horrible nightmares. Along about the second night with no booze I actually had hallucinations. I saw things that couldn't have possibly been there. I think I was maybe half asleep, but can't swear to it. At least I didn't get "snakey" as the old timers I knew in Montana called it when someone would see snakes during his detoxification process. There weren't any pink elephants, but there were some strange things going on in my bedroom that night.

So here I am today, clean and sober and working as a private investigator. All I did to start my business was obtain a license to carry a concealed weapon and had some business cards printed. I started passing them around and before I knew it, I got my first gig. A woman called me and said she suspected her husband of cheating on her. I know, classic gumshoe stuff, right, but that's what happened. So I took the case and followed her husband around for a few days. I was performing surveillance as it's called in the biz. The poor bastard wasn't cheating on his wife at all. He was just working long, hard days as an insurance salesman probably trying to give that bitch wife of his everything she wanted and I have a feeling she wanted a lot. That gig didn't pay much, but the experience convinced me I could be a private investigator.

The second job was a bit more challenging. It seems this man, I'll call him Tom, suspected his business partner had hired a contract killer. Tom was concerned for his life. Tom told me that he wanted to sell the business, and retire, but his partner didn't want to sell and damn sure wasn't ready to retire. Tom offered to sell out to the partner, but the partner didn't have the money. He hadn't been as frugal with his earnings as Tom had been. The partner even looked for someone to buy Tom out, but was unable to find anyone who would pay Tom's asking price, so the business partner told Tom that if he kept trying to sell the business he'd be damn sorry. The guy must have been pretty sincere since Tom came to see me. Even so though, it turned out old Tom was just a little neurotic since he'd been embezzling from the company which the partner suspected all along. Seems old

Tom's gonna be spending a little time in the crowbar hotel. People are so stupid sometimes. Why would he hire a private investigator knowing I might uncover his misdealing?

I've found that this private eye business is done mostly in seedy hotels and bars; the exact places I should probably be staying away from, but its part of the job. My work takes me where the pimps and whores hang out; to the kinds of neighborhoods where gang-bangers, druggies, drunks, and bums live. It's nothing like my old life with the rich clients and partners, classy parties, drinks with little umbrellas, and hors d'oeuvres made with only the best caviar and cheese.

Now its bars that reek of piss, strip joints with strippers who are willing to provide a little value-added service for a little extra moolah, hookers, pimps, and drunks who have shit themselves shitless. It's funny though. I prefer this life to my old one. At least I'm outside much of the time now. I'm not stuck behind a desk getting fat.

It seems that once I was away from the stressful life of a corporate attorney, I didn't feel the need to drink anymore. I didn't feel the pressure to constantly perform, meet deadlines, and quotas. I didn't have to represent some tight ass prick who wasn't satisfied being a millionaire several times over. Oh no. He had to file a law suit against so and so for such and such a reason just so he could earn another several hundred thousand. I really hate greed like that, I mean, yes my cut on a multi-million dollar deal was significant, but I never really felt good taking it. I guess I was never cut out to be a lawyer. In fact, I'd rather have the drunken lowlifes I deal with now. At least you know where you stand with them and they're not all a bunch of greedy bastards.

On the contrary, I've found most of these street people to be quite giving toward one another. They help and protect each other. You don't see that in the corporate world. "Kick 'em when they're down" and "take no prisoners" are the mantras of big business. Just put a partnership up for grabs at a big law firm and see how many friends you have. Lines are drawn in the sand, and the fighters toe the line. People choose sides based on who they think will win the partnership. Friends become foes overnight. That's just how it is. You get used to it, or most people get used to it. I never really did. That's not how it works on the street. Out here, friends stay loyal or die.

So tonight I am on a new case. I'm looking for Trixy Bedluv, a twenty five-year old pole dancer slash hooker who went missing a few days ago. When her pimp, Papa B, hired me to find her, he described her as tall and slim with reddish-blond hair. He said, "She looks like Nicole Kidman, with aftermarket hooters."

Papa B thinks she either hooked up with a sugar daddy and ran away with him, or got herself tangled up with a bad John and is laying dead in a ditch someplace. Either could be true, but according to the pimp, she owes him a pretty healthy chunk of change. Plus, good-earning, healthy whores aren't easy to replace. She was bringing in an easy five hundred a night for him and another two, two fifty a night for herself, more on the weekends. Sometimes she could earn $2,500 in a weekend. Understandably, he wants her back. I think his first scenario is the most likely explanation. She found some rich John who thinks he's found a hooker with a heart of gold. It happens all the time. She'll probably go back to Papa as soon as she's milked old Johnny for all he's worth thinking Papa will forgive her if she's got a fistful of cash for him. In the meantime, I can make a few extra bucks trying to find her.

So there I was searching the sleazy bars and hotels with a picture of this girl asking every lowlife bartender, drug dealer, porn peddler, and prostitute if they know this person or have seen her recently. Some say they've seen her around before but not in a few days. Others don't seem to know her but you get the feeling they are lying. Slippin' 'em a twenty might refresh their memory but you don't trust 'em enough so you move on to the next lowlife. You learn who you can trust to tell you what they know and who is full of shit.

As I continue my search of the shitholes, I spot Simon, or 'Seemoan' as he's known on the street, walking right toward me. He's a little Mexican bastard about five, five. He sells drugs, fences stolen goods, a small time punk who knows everybody. He's usually a valuable snitch for a crisp fifty if I play it cool.

"Hey Seemoan," I call out as he approaches.

"Hey Cabrone," he says his face brightening as he recognizes me. "What's up, dude?"

"Not much, man, just cruisin' you know?"

"Hey Sage, man, you never just cruise. Who you lookin' for bro?"

I pull the picture out of the breast pocket of my jacket. "You recognize this chick?" I ask handing him the photo.

"Ah... Yeah, man, I think so, dude. What'd she do?"

"I'm just looking for her, Simon. You see her lately?"

He holds the picture closer to his eyes, then farther away. "I don't know, man, could be I seen her last night, dude... not sure."

I reach into the same breast pocket and produce a twenty. "Can you be sure now?" I ask handing him the bill.

"Yeah man," he says taking the twenty. "I think I did see her with a white dude. They was leavin' da joint together as I was goin' in."

"What joint was that, Simon?"

"Ah, lemme think... I think it was dah..." I hand him another twenty and he starts stammering again. "You know man, da joint, you know da Rose?"

The Pink Rose, local hangout for drug dealers and prostitutes. "Did you see where they went?"

"Hey man, I ain't nobody's keeper, but I think they went where all Papa's hoes takes 'em: down ta da heartbreak, dude."

"The heartbreak, huh."

"Yeah man, that's where all the hoes from the joint goes."

"Anything else, Simon?" I ask.

"Hey man, you gonna give me another twenty if I say yes?" He smiles that big, spic smile of his and then shakes his head. "No, dude, they ain't no mo." You know all I know now, man."

As he starts walking down the street he looks back and says, "You have a good evening, ah-ight, dude?" I assured him that I would do just that as I began my journey to the Honeymoon Inn, colloquially known as "The Heartbreak Hotel."

Chapter 3

Trixy suddenly became aware of a sharp pain on her inner thigh. It was that fucker who was keeping her prisoner, that Prickface son of a bitch pinching the inside of her thigh, hard! "It's time, bitch," he said with his gravelly voice, "Get that punkass pimp of yours on the horn." She took the phone from his extended hand. "Now!" he growled. She dialed the phone and waited for Papa B to answer. She felt woozy, like she was coming out from under anesthesia after surgery. She felt cold and damp. She suddenly realized she was stark naked lying on an old, worn out single mattress. There were no sheets or blankets, just the bare mattress. Some of the striped material had rotted away allowing the stuffing to poke through. It smelled of old body odor and piss. Why was she naked? What had happened to her? Had she been drugged? She tried to sit up to cover herself, but this prickface son of a bitch put a boot on her chest and pressed her down onto her back. Suddenly Papa B answered the phone. "Papa. Help!" she cried trying unsuccessfully to subdue the panic in her voice.

"Give me that," Prickface said as he grabbed the cell phone from her. "I've got your whore, here" he said. "She's already made me a lot of money." Prickface said and then was silent for a moment. Trixy figured Papa must be talking.

"How?" Prickface asked. Then more silence.

When he spoke again he said, I've run eighteen guys through here already and I got more waiting." He paused a few seconds. "I'd rather sell her back to you while there is still something left to sell."

Trixy was shocked. Eighteen guys he had said. Was that true or was he just trying to scare her? Oh my god! Had they worn rubbers? Why couldn't she remember? "Think, Trixy, think..." She struggled to get control of her thoughts, but her brain was on overload. Eighteen men!   Without any protection?   Oh what kind of disease-ridden assholes had done what to her?

Images crept into her mind. She slowly became aware of the pungent smell of cheap, men's cologne. Where was that coming from? Her chest? Oh my God, her breasts reeked of men's cologne. Oh it was true. Eighteen men had had their way with her over the last... how long had it been? What time was it, what day was it? Where the hell was she?

Prickface, who had been babbling about something, became silent again for a few seconds, bringing Trixy back to reality.

"Yeah," Prickface said suddenly, "I'd say fifty thousand will buy you a brand new... well, let's say, slightly used little whore."

"Fifty thousand?!" Trixy could hear Papa's voice even though Prickface held the phone tight to his ear.

"That's right. I figure this little whore of yours makes a lot of money for you. If she only works five nights a week she's still bringing home twenty five, maybe three grand. I'm only asking for a little taste... and I want it tonight, or you can kiss your little money-maker here good bye. I'll let these fuckin' perverts fuck her to death for $20 each, then dump her wore out ass in the river."

More silence... deafening silence. Finally Prickface spoke again.

"Let me put it this way" he said, a big grin coming over his face. "Right now she's still a prime piece of real estate, maybe not Boardwalk, more like Marvin's Gardens but if you don't pay me what I want tonight, by tomorrow she'll be Baltic Avenue."

With that, he closed his cell phone and looked down at Trixy smiling. "You're gonna make me a bunch of money tonight." he said. "What do you think of that?"

Trixy said nothing. She felt very vulnerable lying there naked on that putrid mattress.

"So" he said, sitting down next to her and grabbing her left breast. "How about you entertain me while we wait?" Trixy tried to brush his hand away but he was too strong. He pinched her hard on her side just below the ribs. She winced in pain, but didn't cry out.

"C'mon, baby" he said. "Don't be shy. Let's have some fun."

Trixy had no intention of being shy. "Fuck you!" she said. He grabbed her nipple and twisted it. She couldn't help herself. She yelled out in pain this time.

"I'll rip your nipples off" he said, laughing. "Is that what you want, bitch?" He kept asking and twisting until she had no choice but to answer. "No" she said. "I will do whatever you want."

He grabbed her behind the head and shoved her face toward his crotch. "You know what I want, baby."

Chapter 4

Just as I was about to enter the Heartbreak, my cell phone went off. I snapped it open and answered.

"Trixy's been kidnapped" Papa said. "Some asshole is holdin' her for ransom. Says he wants fifty thousand tonight or he's gonna mess her up."

"Any idea who he is?" I asked.

"No. But he's a small time punk. Hell, I'd pay twice that to get her back."

"She's worth that much to ya, huh?"

"Hey man, she ain't just my best earner, I love da bitch, you know?" If he loves her so much why does he make her hook? I wondered.

"Any idea where she's being held?" I asked.

"Not really. Man. Maybe da West Bottoms area. That's where he said to meet him."

I had pretty much convinced myself that she had run off with some fat cat John and was milking him for all he was worth. I'd heard stories before of hookers doing an extra John a night, doing six but reporting five. She'd keep the extra money to bankroll a vacation for herself. After a month or two, she could afford a week or ten-day vacation. She'd run off with some rich, older guy and shack up for a while. She'd let the guy buy her jewelry or whatever and live like a normal housewife for a short while. Then when she had the opportunity, she would cut out on the poor fool, taking whatever she could with her. She'd stop at a pawn shop and hawk whatever he'd given her or whatever she'd stolen from him for whatever she could get and go back to the pimp with the wad of cash she'd saved plus whatever she'd made at the pawn shop.

The pimps know their girls take vacations, but as long as they return with as much money as they would have made working, they don't much care. It doesn't really cost the pimps anything as long as the girls aren't arrested for stealing from the Johns. The girls work extra to bankroll the vacation, and the pimps get a good share of it in the end, so what the hell? It beats having them in jail or laid up sick. "Keep the girls happy" is the mantra of most pimps I know.

I was certain this had been one of those situations. I was wrong. I began to question myself. Could I actually handle a real case, a dangerous case? I wasn't sure but I had taken Papa's down payment, so I was in this far. I might as well see how this all plays out. Chances were good that Papa would put up the money and either the kidnapper would return Trixy or she'd wash up along the river somewhere. Either way, my being in immediate danger wasn't much of a concern to me.

"So you're gonna pay the fifty?" I asked.

"Shit yeah man. I gotta deliver it tonight and I want you to come with me."

"What do you need me for?"

"Security, man. You dah only one besides me who knows about this. I ain't got no one else I can trust, man, and I don't wanna go in there alone."

"I'm not really a security guy, you know, Papa."

"You got a gun, don't cha? So I'll double your fee. Meet me at the old industrial warehouse area in the West Bottoms at 3:00 tonight. That's where he wants me to deliver the money."

"I'll be there" I said, but Papa had already hung up. The West Bottoms is the oldest part of Kansas City. The destination of many old west cattle drives. Some of the warehouses are still in operation, but for the most part, the buildings are abandoned. It will be deserted at three in the morning. Man, what had I gotten myself into?

I figured Papa would be armed and so would the kidnapper so I had better bring my .45. If it all went to shit, we'd have an old fashioned shoot out in the West Bottoms. "Wouldn't that be something?" I asked myself out loud. It certainly wouldn't have been the first shootout the West Bottoms had ever seen.

On the other hand, if all goes well, doubling my fee is a pretty nice payday. I figured I'd make six grand on this deal alone. That was enough to subsidize my interest income for the remainder of this year.

My reason for entering the Heartbreak had just been jerked away from me so I turned around and headed for my car. I was getting hungry... might as well get something to eat and then hit the rack until time to meet Papa. It wasn't but 4:30 in the afternoon, but if I got some good sleep I'd be more alert if the shit hit the fan tonight.

"What the hell is life without a little excitement," I asked myself, trying to conjure some courage without applying booze.

As I started my car, I thought about how isolated the West Bottoms is today. Papa was probably right. If the kidnapper wants to meet there, chances are he's holding Trixy somewhere close. He probably wouldn't leave her alone when he came to pick up the money. He would either bring her along, leave her with an accomplice, or kill her before he came to collect the money. Best not to leave witnesses alive. I wondered what kind of personality we were dealing with. Like Papa said, fifty thousand is not a lot of money for a kidnapping, even if the hostage *is* a whore. The prison time for kidnapping would be a pretty long stretch. I couldn't imagine anyone taking the risk for less than a hundred grand myself.

I decided it would be best if I could arrive in the West Bottoms early and see if I could see any light coming from any of the abandoned buildings, but many of the buildings were so old, they weren't wired for electricity. Still, getting there early might give me the edge I need.

I drove home and dug through my fridge for something to eat. I found some left-over lasagna I had made earlier in the week. I nuked it up and ate it in front of the TV. Then I decided I'd better get some sleep. I had a big night ahead of me.

Chapter 5

Trixy still lay naked on the mattress in the dark room. The drugs had finally worn off and she was thinking relatively clearly. She was shivering violently partly because she was cold, but mostly because she believed she was living the last hours of her life cold, hungry, and alone.

A knock came on the door. She was surprised that Prickface would bother to knock. As he entered he said, "OK Hon. It's time to get dressed. We've got a little business meeting."

Did he just call her Hon? Why was he being nice now? He entered the room with a drab, brownish dress. It looked like some kind of print, but in the dim light, Trixy couldn't really tell what color it was. He held a small flashlight. "There's a sink over there" he said illuminating the area with the flashlight. "Here is a wash cloth. Take it and clean yourself up and then put this on." He handed her the dress and flashlight. "I'll be waiting for you out here, so hurry up."

Trixy stood and found her way to the sink. She was surprised to find an unbroken mirror above the sink. She cranked open the faucets and the pipes moaned heavily but produced water, dirty at first, but eventually clearing. The water showed no sign of warming. Probably no hot water heater in this place. She didn't know where she was, but she could tell even in the dim light produced by the flashlight the sink was old. The mirror above it was even older. Not much better than the tin sheets they use as mirrors in some of the rest stops along the highway.

She illuminated the mirror with the flashlight. She looked like hell. She washed her face as best she could with no soap, and when she finished decided she maybe didn't look quite as bad as she'd originally thought. Still, she wished she had some make up.

"Hurry up in there!" Prickface shouted from the other side of the door.

"I'm almost ready" she muttered.

Trixy held up the bland, drab dress. This was it? What about underwear? This ugly dress is all she got to wear?

Trixy slipped into the dress and shown the flashlight on it. Looking in the mirror she saw the dress was some kind of brown or tan with white flower print. "Where are my clothes?" she asked but Prickface didn't answer. "Shoes?" Where were her shoes? As she opened the door she asked Prickface if she could have her shoes.

"You won't need shoes where you're going, or socks either for that matter." That statement chilled her to the bone. Did he mean she'd be dead soon? She chased the idea out of her head. "I could sure use a smoke... could I borrow one?"

"Like cigars, Toots? That's what I smoke."

"Sure" she said. At this point she'd smoke horse shit if it would calm her nerves. "They've got nicotine in them, right?" she asked.

He unwrapped a cheap cigar handed it to Trixy and offered a light. "You know," he said, "I was the first guy to have you in there. Do you remember?"

"I don't really remember much of anything" she said. "It's all kind of a blur."

"Well your weren't much of a fuck just laying there... I might want another go at you sometime when this is all over. You'd give an old friend a freebie, right?" he said touching her face with a hand the size of a catcher's mitt. She grabbed his wrist before he could touch her. He slapped her hard with his other hand. "You'll do me any time I want, bitch... That is if you are still alive after tonight."

"God what a bastard this guy is" she thought. He knew she was scared shitless, as it was, shaking so hard she could barely get the cigar to her mouth and rather than try to console here her, he made it worse. She wanted to scream. She wanted to shoot the fucker in the head. God she hoped Papa would shoot this bastard. But not kill him. She wanted to spit in his dying eyes and tell him he fucked with the wrong girl. She wanted to beat his face to an unrecognizable pulp before he died. The thought was turning her fear into anger. She began to feel more courageous as anger replaced fear. It felt good.

"Are you ready?" he asked.

"I'd feel better if I had shoes" she said.

Ignoring her comment, he grabbed her by the arm and said, "Let's go."

He led her out the front door of the old abandoned building, down a flight of old, chipped, concrete steps and out onto the street. Trixy chanced a glance over her shoulder. She made out the words, "Kansas City Bolt Nut" before Prickface jerked on her arm and made her turn around. After crossing the street, they entered an old, abandoned street. Another street ran above turning the old street into a kind of tunnel. She didn't see any street signs. She had no idea where they were. The lower street, the street they were walking down, looked as though it hadn't been used in decades. She imagined the last car to drive down this street was a 1966 Thunderbird convertible. Her father had a car like that, and right now she wished she were in it driving away from this nightmare.

There was no one else around. The only sound was Prickface's shoes scuffling along the old pavement, kicking an occasional rock now and then. There were streetlights to her left, but most had burned out long ago. The street they had crossed before entering the tunnel ran parallel with the old street under the tunnel where they were walking. Trixy figured Prickface wanted to stay under as much cover as he could.

Suddenly he tugged on her arm and they left the relative safety of the tunnel toward another street that ran away from the tunnel street. They were approaching an old, brick building that sort of reminded her of her grade school. The only thing missing was the long, covered fire escape slide.

This building was six stories high, with huge garage doors allowing access to the bottom level. As they got closer to the building, Trixy made out the words "CRANE CO" above the entrance to the building.

"Are we going in there?" she asked. "There could be gangsters in there."

Prickface didn't answer. He just kept walking toward the building and pulling her along. Soon they were standing before the front doors of the building. The doors looked out of place. They looked like doors that belonged on a much newer building. They were metal-framed, glass doors, and miraculously the glass was unbroken, at least it was up until Prickface got to them. He tried the doors. They were locked. Prickface pulled a pistol from the back of his pants and swung wildly at the glass doors. With a loud smash, the glass in one door shattered. Trixy wondered how long the glass had been there.

He ducked and passed under the chards of glass hanging from the top of the door frame, then jerked her through roughly. Had she not ducked just in the nick of time, she'd have run her face into a jagged edge of glass protruding from the left part of the frame.

It was dark and dank inside the building. "If there are ghosts anywhere in this city, here is where most of them hang out" Trixy thought.

They went up a flight of stairs to the second floor so they could watch out the windows for Papa. Most of the windows were boarded up, but finally Trixy found one that wasn't. She took up a position in front of it and looked out onto the street below. Not a car or pedestrian in sight anywhere. Her anger had disappeared. She was beginning to feel fearful again. She longed for someone to come along, anyone. She'd even welcome the site of a gang at this point. Things were looking bleak. She continued to watch out the window for ten minutes or so.

Suddenly she saw dim lights that seemed to be approaching from several blocks down the street. She could not see a car, or even the lights directly, just their reflection off the street. They seemed to be getting closer.

"Think that's him?" asked Prickface.

"I don't know... maybe."

Suddenly the lights went out. Trixy had never spotted the vehicle itself.

"What the hell?" asked Prickface. They watched quietly waiting for someone to appear from the shadows. Prickface pulled his cell phone from his shirt pocket and handed it to Trixy. "Call your pimp and see where he is."

She took the phone, dialed the number and waited for Papa to answer. She didn't have to wait long. Papa answered on the second ring.

"Papa?" said Trixy. Prickface ripped the phone from her hand and held it to his ear. "Where the fuck are you?"

"I just left home. It's not even two-thirty yet. I'll be there by three. Don't worry."

"You better be."

"I will... Where exactly do you want me to go?"

"Are you sure you're not here already?"

"No. I am just getting on I-70."

"Well there's someone else here. You didn't tell anybody about our meeting, did you?"

"No suh, I want my Trixy back safe and sound"

"You have my number now. You call me when you get in the neighborhood and I'll direct you from there."

Prickface hung up without response to Papa's last statement. When he'd told Papa he'd get his little tramp back, he'd been lying. Trixy was done, and so was Papa. He couldn't risk leaving a witness that had seen him as close up as Trixy had. He'd collect the money from Papa and shoot them both dead and that would be that. All he had to do was wait for Papa to show, but he couldn't help but wonder who else was nosing around the West Bottoms this time of night.

Chapter 6

I parked my car and observed my surroundings for about five minutes. The area was a real slum. Mine was the only car on the streets anywhere in this shitty neighborhood. The West Bottoms is even uglier and desolate than I remembered.

The entire area seemed to have been constructed from concrete and brick. There were several dilapidated redbrick buildings in various stages of decomposition. Many still standing but looking like hollow shells that could at any moment collapse into a pile of rubble. Here and there an abandoned house probably domiciles for the families of the factory workers who labored for countless hours in some assembly line for little pay. The faint smell of old mixed with mold and sulfur hit my nose.

Nobody hangs out here anymore. Even the gangs don't want it. There is nothing here. A person could die here and rot to nothing but a bleached-out skeleton before anyone would find him.

I opened the car door as quietly as possible and slipped out carefully closing the door behind me. In that kind of silence, the slightest sound is magnified ten-fold. I was across the street from a dilapidated building with "Langdon Supply Co." printed on the side. There was a yard between the street and the building surrounded by a high chain-link fence with three strands of barbed wire at the top. It looked formidable. The whole yard sat on a concrete slab about 5 feet high. Old, washed out gang graffiti was still visible on the side of the concrete facing me. Obviously there had been gang activity here at one time, but not anymore. I wondered if the gang who had written the graffiti still existed or was as long gone as life itself from this place. Usually when someone mentions a ghost town, I tend to think of a town in the old west, but this was as much a ghost town as any western ghost town I'd ever seen.

I crept up to the concrete wall and hunkered down behind it. I looked up and down the street searching for something; I wasn't sure what, maybe movement, anything that might give me an idea as to where we were meeting this kidnapper.

Staying low, I crept around the corner of the high concrete wall and paused to look around. There were no visible signs of life in any direction. I stayed low and waited. Papa should be coming soon, I thought.

Finally I saw car lights approaching. He was coming down the same street I had. Surely he'd notice my car parked on the other side of the street. The car slowed to a crawl as it approached. It seemed to take an eternity for him to get to where my car was parked. Once he finally did, he gunned the engine and drove past without stopping. He hooked a right at the next street.

I waited impatiently for several minutes waiting for his car to come back around. It was taking him so long, I was beginning to wonder if it had been Papa at all? Maybe it had been some gangsters scoping my vehicle. Suddenly I saw movement behind my car. It was one person alone, staying low. Papa must have parked his car a block over and crept up on foot.

I wanted to be certain it was actually Papa before revealing my whereabouts. I waited, watching... He waited, also watching. Suddenly, like he had been fired from a cannon Papa raced across the street to the same place I had originally ran to when I left my car. I was certain he hadn't spotted me yet. He must have assumed I was somewhere in close proximity considering the location of my vehicle.

I crept toward the corner thinking he would wait for me, but instead he appeared just as I was about to make my move around the corner. We startled each other when we both appeared at the same time at the corner, but made no noise. When he spoke, it was in a whisper so low, it was barely audible.

"He called me" he said breathlessly.

"When?" I asked.

"About twenty minutes ago. I was on my way. I thought I was running early."

"What did he say?"

"He said someone else was nosing around the neighborhood. I figured he spotted you. Any chance you've been made?"

"I don't know. I can't see how unless he saw my headlights."

"I think that's probably what he saw, but he's got no reason other than paranoia to believe there's anyone with me. It's not like I'm gonna call the cops to help me save my best girl."

"OK... So what do we do now?" I asked.

"I'm supposed to call him when I get here."

I tilted my head in a "go for it" motion.

He pulled his cell phone from his pocket, pushed send, then send again. He didn't wait long for a response.

"OK," he said. "I am here."

I couldn't hear what the kidnapper was saying even in the absolute silence of our environment. Papa must have kept the volume on his phone turned down low.

"Yeah" he said, that was my car... The one earlier? I have no idea. Like I told you I--" He stopped talking abruptly. The kidnapper must have cut him off. I heard the word "Bullshit" and "...body with you" faintly over Papa's phone.

"No," Papa said, "I am alone." Papa didn't speak for a few seconds. The kidnapper was keeping his voice low so I was unable to hear any more of his side of the conversation over Papa's phone.

"OK," Papa said finally. "Give me a few minutes and I'll be there." He snapped his phone shut, looked at me and said, "Follow me, but keep out of sight."

Staying low, he walked along the concrete wall away from the corner. We walked about fifty feet before Papa stopped and motioned for me to come closer.

"He's up this way" he said, "in a building marked "Crane Co... know where it is?"

I shook my head. "No" I mouthed.

"I don't either, but it's up this street a block or two. Once we cross the side street up ahead, he could be in any of those old warehouses. I have no idea which is the Crane building."

I nodded my acknowledgement.

"You're gonna have to stay behind me a good way, but keep me in sight. OK?"

"I'll find a hiding place where I can keep an eye on you, block by block" I said.

He nodded. "I'll give you a sign when I find em... Or he finds me."

"What kinda sign?" I asked.

"I don't know, man, but you'll recognize it when you see it." Without further conversation he started for the end of the block staying as close to the concrete wall as possible. I followed about fifty feet behind.

There wasn't much cover in this desolate place, but there wasn't much light either allowing for many shadows I could hide beneath and stay pretty much out of sight. I came to a corner and waited. I crossed the street about fifteen seconds after Papa and lucked out by finding a concrete staircase that led to an entrance to a building below street level. I quickly scrambled down them. The height wasn't ideal. I had to stand on my tiptoes to keep an eye on Papa.

Without looking back at me, Papa took a big breath and stepped out onto the street and walked slowly toward an old warehouse with "CRANE CO" written on the side in big block letters. It was no different from the rest of the brick buildings in this area, other than it looked a bit sturdier. Many of the buildings looked as though they would collapse in a strong wind, but this one somehow looked stronger.

Papa strolled along swinging his duffel bag full of money as if he were a sight-seer on vacation. I pulled my .45 and racked it as quietly as I could. I wished I'd had a rifle with a powerful scope. A .45 ain't much good for anything but up close work.

I watched Papa saunter down the street. When he was about to cross the next side street, I made my move. I couldn't just walk down the sidewalk though. There was too much light and not enough cover, so I climbed out of the staircase, ran around the corner behind me and dashed for the alley. I hoped the alley went all the way to the end of the block.

Upon reaching the alley, I saw that it did go all the way down the block toward the Crane Co. Building. I ran for all I was worth to the end of the alley trying to stay in the shadows. As I approached the side street, I slowed and angled to my right leaning against the brick wall of another building and inched my way toward the sidewalk outside the alley opening.

I heard Papa before I saw him. He was walking rather nosily, stepping heavily and kicking rocks as he went. I figured he must have wanted to be heard because I had witnessed firsthand how stealthily he could move when he wanted to. Maybe he was trying to cover the noise I had made scrambling down the alley.

I heard a voice call out from the Crane Building. "Over here." Papa stopped mid-stride and looked up toward the sound.

"You looking to get rid of that bag you're packin?" the voice asked.

"I'm looking to trade this bag if you got what I want" Papa said.

I could see Papa, but I couldn't see what Papa saw because he was slightly ahead of me looking to his left. I was slightly behind him and a half a block to his left at the entrance of the alley. I wasn't sure I could move safely. I waited for his signal.

I heard the man in the building say "Is this what you're looking for?"

I guess the kidnapper must have shoved Trixie's face to the window because Papa's expression turned to that of concern.

"Throw down your gun" the kidnapper commanded.

"I ain't armed" Papa said setting the bag on the street and raising his hands in the air. As he did, he flicked his wrist twice. As subtle as the move was, I took it as my cue. He must have seen Trixy and was signaling me that she was there and that I should move. At least I hoped that's what he meant. I crossed the street and melded into the shadow of the wall of the Crane Building. I began creeping toward the corner of the building where Papa stood. I figured the kidnapper was paying close attention to Papa, especially after his setting the bag down and raising his hands. He might have thought Papa was trying to pull something.

"All right," the voice said. "So you ain't armed... How do I know you ain't lying?"

"All I want is my Trixy back. I ain't packing. I swear to it."

I inched closer to the corner of the building. Papa was standing in the middle of the street about ten feet ahead of me. I couldn't see him, but I was listening to the conversation.

"Just meet me at the door, and I'll trade you this bag for Trixy."

"Not so fast, Papa. I need to be sure you aren't armed."

There was a slight pause in the conversation. I figured the kidnapper was trying to think of a way for Papa to prove he was unarmed. "Take your clothes off" the kidnapper said suddenly. "All of em."

"I told you, I ain't packin."

"Take em off!" the voice shouted.

I couldn't see anything, but I knew Papa must be stripping in the middle of the street. I inched closer to the corner as quietly as I could. Papa must be wondering where the hell I was.

"Skivvies too" the voice said.

"What do you think; this is a pistol in my underwear?" Papa said.

"Just want to be sure" the voice responded, "For all I know, you're packin a python in there."

As I approached the corner of the building, I wondered, do I dare a glance? With my body as far behind me as I could get it, I slowly moved my head around the corner. I saw Papa standing in the street buck naked with his hands in the air.

"Turn around" the voice commanded. Papa obeyed.

"Pick up the bag with one hand."

Papa reached down with one hand, the other still in the air, and lifted the bag. Standing there naked, holding the bag, he chanced a glance at the corner of the building. I don't think he saw me although I was watching.

"Unzip the bag and empty it on the street."

Papa did as he was told. Money fell out of the bag onto the street. Papa said, "This bag doesn't have any other pockets in it."

"Throw it away then." The voice commanded.

Papa flung the bag straight down the street opposite of me.

"All right," the voice said, "Now come in the building. The entrance is on the side street over there. You come up and then we'll all leave together."

Papa reached down to pick up his clothes.

"Leave em," said the voice. You can get em later. Sides, you ain't got nothin this bitch ain't seen before."

"What about the money."

"Leave it too."

I thought that was strange. Why would he want Papa to just leave fifty thousand dollars in the street? What if a wind came up?

Anyway, Papa was coming and I wasn't sure what I should do. The front entrance to the building was behind me. I decided to wait for Papa at the corner of the building and exchange places with him as he passed. I inched up closer to the corner and waited. Papa came around the corner and our eyes met. "Shoot the fucker" he said in a low voice as he passed me, his dark skin glistening in the moonlight.

I darted around the corner and waited, my .45 held close to my chest. I heard Papa knock on the front door. I heard a creaking sound as the door opened. I heard Papa say, "Let's get the money before it blows away." Then I heard the kidnapper tell Papa to step back. Then nothing, then a loud pop, pop, pop, followed by a scream. I brought my head around the corner to find Papa spread out on the sidewalk below the entrance to the building, blood pooling around his head. Standing there on the steps was a huge figure, still pointing his gun where Papa had been standing, barrel smoking. "Let's go collect the money" he said reaching for the girl.

"Oh Papa" Trixy shouted running toward the naked, broken body on the sidewalk. The kidnapper reached for her again, but she was out of range. She flew down the stairs to Papa. The kidnapper leveled his pistol at her and said "I don't need you anymore, anyway."

I took aim, but my .45 was in my left hand, the rest of my body hidden behind the building. I usually couldn't hit shit left-handed, but I fired anyway. The man recoiled and I knew I'd hit him but he recovered quickly and aimed at me. I darted back around the corner just in time. A bullet hit the side of the building and ricocheted tearing chunks of brick and mortar with it. If I'd been standing there, I'd have been hit by the barrage. I waited a couple of seconds then chanced another glance around the corner. The big man was gone. Trixy was bent beside Papa holding his head in her lap and sobbing uncontrollably.

I scanned the surrounding area, but there was no sign of the man. I ran toward Trixy and Papa. Trixy was shouting at me hysterically. "Do something! Give him mouth to mouth or CPR or something!"

I knelt beside Papa. He was gone. There was no resuscitating him. The back of his head had been blown away by two bullets. The third shot must have missed him, but there was a bullet hole beside his nose and one in his forehead. I rolled his head to the side and saw the combined exit wounds were huge. The size of a beer can. His blood was spilling out onto the sidewalk, running off the curb and onto the street. He'd lost most all his blood already. "He's gone, Trixy" I said.

"No, no he can't be."

I stood and looked around. I was pretty concerned that the shooter might still be there somewhere. I suddenly remembered the money. I turned and ran back around the corner. The money that Papa had dumped on the street and his clothes were gone. I ran back to Trixy. "Come on." I said "let's get the hell outta here."

"We can't just leave him." Trixy shouted. "We can't just leave him here naked!"

I extended my left hand, right hand still filled with the .45 ready to fire at whatever moved.

"He's dead, Trixy" I said, "There's nothing more we can do for him." I reached for her and she'd grabbed my hand. I pulled her to her feet.

"We can't just leave him here. He's naked for Christ's sake."

"I doubt he'll mind" I said calmly. "Besides we have no choice at the moment. We're sitting ducks if we stay here. Let's go!"

We ran down the street toward my car leaving Papa's naked body to be found by whoever frequents this place in the daylight.

We ran across the street past the abandoned brick buildings, on a sidewalk that was heaving and broken. We crossed another street and ran past the tall concrete wall Papa and I had hid under only minutes ago. A spark flew from the concrete wall, and then another. I realized we were being shot at. I ran faster. Trixy was stumbling behind me trying to keep up. I stopped before crossing the street that lay between the high concrete wall and my car. I looked down and realized that Trixy had no shoes. I felt really bad for her suddenly. She had run barefoot across pavement, gravel, and broken concrete in her bare feet to get here, all without complaining even once. Her clothes were covered in Papa's blood. I realized she had no idea who I was, where we were going or how much farther she'd have to run. I looked at her before crossing the street. "It'll all be over soon" I said. That's my car across the street."

We dashed toward my car. Luckily I'd left it unlocked just in case. I almost hadn't because I was worried about theft but right then I was really glad I didn't have to stop and fumble with keys.

I fired her up, whipped a U-turn and with tires squealing, we got the hell out of there. I didn't turn on the headlights right away because I didn't want to give him a better target, but I didn't let the throttle off the floor until we hit 60 either. Once we had traveled a safe distance, I slowed down to within the speed limit and looked over at Trixy who was shaking uncontrollably.

"So who the hell are you?" she asked. "And what were you doing there?"

"I'm a private investigator. Papa hired me to help him find you. He said he'd give me three thousand dollars for your safe return."

"Oh poor Papa. He's dead. Papa B is dead." I didn't answer. I didn't know what to say so I just remained quiet and drove. Neither of us spoke for a good while.

"I hit him," I said finally wanting to break the silence.

"What?" she asked without looking at me.

"The kidnapper. I'm pretty sure I hit him when I shot."

"But you didn't kill him!" she said angrily. "Now what the hell am I going to do?" She sagged and held her head in her hands. "Oh God, what will I do now?" she asked sobbing into her hands.

Again I found myself at a loss for words. I thought knowing that I had a least wounded the fucker might be of some consolation to her, but it obviously wasn't. I was afraid to say anything more. She'd been through a very harrowing ordeal. She was probably on the verge of a nervous breakdown. I couldn't think of anything to say that might help, so I said nothing.

After a long silence Trixy spoke. "Will you take me to your place?" she asked.

"My place? Why my place?"

"I have nowhere else to go."

"Don't you have friends or family where you could go?"

"No. Papa was all I had. He treated me really good. Always saved the best guys for me. Never anything dangerous. Oh Papa." she cried. I could see she was completely grief-stricken, like she'd just lost her father or husband. I said nothing for a few more seconds. I just drove and thought about the situation. I had just risked my life for three thousand lousy dollars... Three thousand that I would never see and now I was stuck with a prostitute I couldn't in good conscience dispose of. I didn't really have room for company at my small apartment. I tried to come up with other ideas.

"I could put you up in a hotel for a while." I suggested.

"Oh sure." she said coldly, "just like every other man. When you're done with me, just dump me off somewhere." She looked over at me and touched my right arm lightly. "What's your name?" she asked.

"Chandler" I answered. "Sage Chandler."

"Well Sage Chandler?" she started in a cooing voice, "I am afraid to stay at a hotel by myself. I don't want to be alone tonight. Let me come home with you and I'll make it worth your while." It was already not worth my while. I doubted she could change that. I looked at her. She looked scared. I thought about her running down the street in bare feet. I thought about what might have happened to her while she was held captive. I felt sorry for her again.

"There's no need for that, Trixy." I said. "You can come home with me tonight and we'll sort things out tomorrow."

"Thank you, Sage." she said, then scooted over beside me and kissed my cheek. "Thank you very much" she whispered before laying her head on my shoulder.

Chapter 7

"What the hell happened, Max?" Hughie asked. "Are you hurt bad?"

"There was somebody else there tonight." Max answered as he dropped the duffel bag and an armload of clothing and made his way to a broken down easy chair in his ill furnished apartment.

"What? Who?"

"I don't know who, but Papa brought someone else with him and the fucker shot me." Hughie rushed to his side and looked at the wounded bicep. "That don't look good to me, Max." he said. "But let's get that shirt off and let me take a closer look." He unbuttoned Max's shirt and began to gingerly pull at the sleeve. Max howled in pain. Hughie decided the best thing was to cut the sleeve off. He raced to the kitchen and returned with a pair of scissors.

"I'm gonna cut it off, Max, so it won't hurt so much."

Max relaxed his arm and allowed Hughie to remove the sleeve with the scissors. Hughie skillfully cut around the sleeve as close to the shoulder as possible. He was very careful not to touch Max's left bicep. Once he had the sleeve cut all around, he cut it up the back side and unfolded it around Max's arm. He examined the wound carefully.

"Oh that ain't good, Boss" he said. I don't see an exit wound. I think the bullet is still in there somewhere."

"So?" Max said "Take it out."

"Oh I can't do that, Max. We gotta get you to a doctor."

"No doctors" Max said grimacing. "You do it."

"I can't Max. I'll do more damage digging the bullet out."

Max slumped into his chair. "You gotta do it Hughie. I can't go to a doctor. They'll arrest me if they run a check on me... You know that!"

"But..." Hughie stammered, "I might fuck it up worse, Boss. You might lose your arm."

"Well just stop the bleeding and bandage it up. We'll leave the damn bullet in there." Hughie's face turned solemn.

"Can't." he said, "If we don't get it out, it'll get infected and if it gets infected, chances are you'll lose the arm."

"Fuck!," Max shouted, "If you dig around in there, it might get worse. If we don't get the bullet out, I lose my arm. Either way, I'm fucked." Max let his head roll to the side. Hughie thought for a second that Max had passed out. "Boss?" he asked. No response. "Max?" Finally Max turned his head toward Hughie. "Did you buy any whiskey, Hughie?" he asked.

"Yeah Boss, I just bought two bottles today, just like you said."

"Bring me some whiskey Hughie and I'll tell you about my night."

"OK Max, but we gotta get something done about your arm tonight."

"Later... Whiskey first."

Hughie went to the kitchen and returned with a bottle of Wild Turkey and two short glasses. Holding one glass with two fingers while resting the other glass in the crook of his elbow, he filled a glass almost to the top and handed it to Max. Then he sat down on a footstool beside Max's chair, filled his own glass and waited for Max to relay his story.

Max seemed to be enjoying his refreshment which delayed the telling of his tale. Hughie, being short on patience couldn't wait for Max to start. "So is that the money?" he asked pointing to the duffel bag. "Did you get the money?"

"Yeah" Max said, "I got the fucking money, Hughie, but just barely." Max drained his glass and motioned to Hughie for a refill. Once the contents of the glass had been replenished, Max began to recount his story.

"I told Papa that I'd introduced eighteen guys to that whore of his while I had her, you know? Just to scare him? It's not true. I was the only one that fucked her. I fucked her twice, but that was it." Max drained his glass and asked for more.

"Then tonight I saw that cocksucker, Papa, coming down the street, swinging that duffel bag like he was going to a Sunday Social. I should have been suspicious, then, God damn it." He took another long drink.

"When he got there, I hollered out the window at him. I thought the little fucker was gonna shit himself." Max moved in his chair and grimaced in pain.

"I made the little bastard strip naked right there in the street." Max laughed at that. Remembering Papa standing there naked struck him as hilarious, but laughing hurt his arm, so his jocularity was short-lived.

"Then I told him to go around the corner to where the front doors are, you know?" Max lifted his glass and swirled the liquid around apparently satisfied with Hughie's choice. "I grabbed that little whore and hauled her downstairs" he said. "When we got down to the doors, there was that fucking Papa, buck naked not more than 6 feet away from me. I shoved the whore through the door first. Then I looked at that fucking Papa and all I could think was shoot the fucker. So I shot him right in his fuckin' face. I shot him three times. Blew him right off the stairs. I saw the blood and brains and shit come out the back of his head. I know I killed him... Fucker."

Max held his glass out indicating to Hughie that he wanted more whiskey. Hughie obliged. "Then that bitch whore got away from me on the steps and went down to tend to Papa. I figured fuck it I'll shoot her too and I was about to do it when this other fucker, whoever he was, shot me in the arm. God Damn it! I returned fire, but I missed the bastard."

Max guzzled another half glass of whiskey. "I'm gonna get drunk, Hughie, and then you're gonna take this bullet outta my arm." He drained his glass and indicated that Hughie should refill it. As Hughie poured, Max continued with his story.

After Max was shot, he didn't hang around long. "I still should have shot that little whore" he said. Instead, he went back in the building. He had scoped the place out the night before when the whore was knocked out on the drugs Hughie had given him to keep her under control. He searched the Crane building and finally found a door that led to one of those cement staircases outside, at basement level. He made sure it was open just in case he needed an escape.

"Man I'm glad I did cause I needed it tonight."

After he realized he'd be shot, Max ducked back inside the Crane building. He made his way through the building and found the basement door leading outside. He had scrambled up those cement steps and ran for the duffel bag. He grabbed up the money and Papa's clothes, and stuffed everything in the duffel bag, and then he ran back down the cement stairs and hid out, waiting. He sipped his whiskey.

"Then that fucker that shot me came racing around the corner. He looked around and went right back again. I couldn't get a shot off. He was just too quick."

Max looked at his arm bleakly, like he'd already accepted the fact that he'd be losing the arm, but he continued his story.

"I thought for a second I could shoot him right in the nuts cause I was directly below him, you know? But he was gone so fast, I didn't get a chance. Then they fucked around a while deciding what to do with Papa. Finally they just left him there and then I seen 'em running down the street. I managed to get a couple shots off but I don't think I hit anything."

Max sat back in his chair and said, "Damn it, Hughie, this fucker is starting to hurt pretty good. You about ready to go after that bullet?"

Hughie didn't want to do it. He'd been a Medic in the Gulf War and had seen many gunshot wounds, but all he'd ever done was field dress them and send the guys off in a helicopter. They didn't perform surgery in the field. Oh he'd helped out in an Army hospital for a few weeks and had assisted in surgeries but he was not trained for something like this. He was sure Max's humerus would be broken, maybe beyond repair. He pleaded with Max.

"Don't make me do it, Boss" he said. "I'm not trained for this kind of thing."

Max insisted. "Come on, Hughie" Max said. "I know you can do it. You have nitrous. I've seen it. That shit puts a guy down, right?"

Hughie took a couple shots of whiskey to soothe his own nerves. "Yeah, but that shit can be dangerous if you don't have the right gauges."

"You can do it, Hughie" Max pleaded. "I know you can."

Finally Hughie agreed. After Max had passed out from drink, he'd attempt to dig the bullet out, but only if Max would retire to his bed before he had any more to drink. Hughie didn't think he could operate on Max's arm while he was sitting in the easy chair, and he knew damn well he couldn't carry Max to bed. Max agreed and Hughie helped him hobble to bed.

Hughie went to a room in the back of the house and brought back a bottle of nitrous oxide and a bottle of oxygen. He'd rigged up a mask that would allow him to administer nitrous and oxygen at the same time or individually whichever he needed.

While Hughie prepared his equipment, Max continued his heavy whiskey consumption. Now and then Hughie would sneak a few more sips of whiskey to keep his nerves steady. Finally Max passed out. He'd been muttering something about getting that asshole that shot him and then he was snoring. "It's show time." Hughie said to himself.

Hughie strapped the mask over Max's face and turned on the nitrous. He knew that alcohol alone will not keep a person under once intense pain is introduced, but with the help of the nitrous, maybe Max would stay under. He hoped to hell he would, because he couldn't imagine how things might go if Max woke up in the middle of the operation.

Hughie knew in his own mind that he would be unable to get the bullet out. He didn't have the expertise or experience for this kind of surgery. He wasn't even sure how much nitrous a man Max's size could withstand, especially with all the whiskey he'd had.

Hughie rolled Max over onto his right side, exposing his left arm. He then unrolled his surgical kit. It resembled a wrench kit like some guys have with different sized wrenches in each pocket, except Hughie's surgical kit had different sized scalpels, forceps, tweezers and such. He pulled out a scalpel and looked at the wound but he was unable to see well enough. He set the scalpel aside and rifled through his kit until he found his favorite invention. It was something he'd fashioned himself that once in position on his head, sported a very bright spotlight and a 10x magnifying glass on a swivel that could be positioned before his left eye.

"That's better" he said aloud.

He reached for the scalpel and began the incision, half expecting Max to wake up, but he didn't. He cut an incision from Max's shoulder to just below the bottom of the wound. He cut through skin and muscle finally exposing the bone itself. He spread the incision as wide as possible with his fingers. The damage the bullet had done was tremendous. As he suspected, it was lodged in the bone, but worse than that, it had mushroomed and splintered the bone. It was all mashed together with bone and muscle, entangled.

Hughie knew he didn't have the tools or expertise to extract it. Now Hughie wasn't sure what to do. If he stitched the wound, the doctors would have to reopen it, but if he left it open and Max refused a doctor, then what?

Hughie thought briefly about taking his scalpel and slicing Max's throat. He could cut the main arteries in the neck and Max would bleed to death in his sleep. Even if he did wake up, he wouldn't last long enough to do anything. He held his scalpel to Max's neck. He even touched it to his skin.

"All I gotta do is press a little and pull" he thought, "and this fucker will be out of my hair forever. But his conscience got the better of him. Hughie had never killed anyone, not even in the Gulf War, and he wasn't about to start now even though he'd never known anyone who needed killing any more than Max did.

He decided to stitch up the incision. That way, if Max chose to go to the hospital, it wouldn't take much for them to remove the stitches. If he chose not to, then the wound would heal better if it were stitched.

Chapter 8

Trixy and I reached my place out 5:30 am. It was still dark and I was dead tired. Trixy was still carrying on about Papa. "I can't believe he's dead" she said. "I have no one else in this whole world. What am I going to do?"

"Well" I began, "first we'll get some sleep and then we can decide what to do. Things won't look so bleak after you've had some sleep."

"Oh it won't matter" she cried. "I'm fucked any way you look at it, tired or rested, I am fucked."

We got out of the car and I helped Trixy up the steps to my front door. Judging by the way she walked, her feet were pretty sore.

"First thing we'd better do is have a look at your feet" I said.

Once inside I told Trixy to sit on the couch and put her feet on my lap. I examined them both. There were little rocks and pieces of concrete embedded in them.

"I've got to clean these up" I said, "or they might become infected." I lowered her feet and went to my medicine cabinet for a hot wash cloth, soap, some iodine, and antibiotic ointment. I returned and began cleaning her wounds.

"This might sting a little, Trixy" I warned.

"Trixy," she said, coughing out the name. "That's not my real name, you know... You think my real name is Trixy Bedlove"

"I was never told your last name."

"Well it's not Bedlove, I'll tell you that much. Bedlove is the name Papa gave me. He thought it sounded like a good name for an exotic dancer. He loved to get on the microphone at the club and say, 'And now, dancing for your pleasure, Miss Trixy Bedlove'. He thought it sounded sexy I guess."

While I continued doctoring her feet, she continued talking. "Wanna know my real name?" she asked.

"If you want to tell me, sure."

"Its... Ouch! That hurt."

"Sorry" I said swabbing her feet with the wash cloth. "Gotta be done."

"My real name is Samantha Johnson."

"No shit? Really?" I asked, trying to sound sincerely interested.

"No shit... Samantha Rhey Johnson, from Bismarck, North Dakota."

I had finished cleaning her feet by then and was applying the iodine and antibiotic ointment. I knew she hadn't finished telling me about herself, but I also knew she was waiting for me to ask, so I did. "So how did a nice girl from North Dakota end up a hook... dancer in Kansas City?"

"You can say it, Sage. I'm a hooker. Not proud of it, but that's what I am. You got anything to drink?"

I found her nonchalance about her profession very intriguing. "What would it be like to have sex for a living?" I wondered, "Especially if you're a woman?" On one hand I could see the attraction, but that was from a man's point of view. On the other hand, I thought most women would find such behavior abhorring, but I wasn't a woman and therefore not qualified to judge. I liked this girl. She had a lot of spunk.

"I might have something" I said. "Nothing with alcohol, though. I don't drink alcohol."

I was lying. I had been keeping an unopened bottle of Gentleman Jack, first generation in a kitchen cupboard. Last I looked it was worth about $80. I'd heard about people who couldn't quit smoking unless they had a pack of cigarettes lying around. I guess that's the way it was with me and alcohol, and I'd had it for several years. I didn't really want to open it now.

"You don't drink?" she mused. "I don't know if I can trust a man who don't drink, even if he is Superman."

"Superman?" I laughed. "Not quite."

"Well, you are my Superman. You saved my ass tonight. If you hadn't been there, I'd be dead now too."

I thought about continuing my lie about the Gentleman Jack. I don't like lying, not even to a stranger like Trixy... Er... Samantha, but I didn't really want to part with my bottle either. I was superstitious about it. I'd had it a long time.

Down deep I had always believed that when that bottle was opened, I'd be the one drinking it, or maybe my children, to commemorate my life after I was gone.

I considered whether to open the bottle for Samantha or not. She was only a whore, but I liked her. I felt like she had earned a drink or two tonight after all she'd been through, but mostly, I wanted to drink with her. The time had come to test myself I decided.

"Actually" I said, "I might have something in a kitchen cabinet. Is whiskey OK?"

"Whiskey would be marvelous" she said.

I went to the kitchen and found the bottle. It was dusty to say the least. I took the bottle down and uncorked the top. It smelled terrific but made me want to gag at the same time. I wanted some, but on the other hand, I didn't. "Want ice?" I asked.

"Please" she said, "but just a couple cubes and maybe a splash of 7-Up if you have it, otherwise water is fine."

Knowing she would spoil a good whiskey with 7-Up was almost enough to ask her to leave my apartment; of course, she didn't know I had the good stuff. Besides, I didn't have any 7-Up. I found some old ice in a tray that had been there for probably a year. It was pretty frosty, but I figured what the hell? Its Ice. I filled a rocks glass with ice, poured a healthy dose of whiskey into the glass, with just a splash of water and delivered it to her.

"So tell me about Bismarck" I said.

"Well" she said, "there's not much to tell really. I was born there, went to school there and left when I was eighteen."

"Does it get cold there?"

She laughed heartily. "How does forty below sound to you?" She took a sip of her drink. "Oh," she exclaimed, "That's' good. What is that?"

"A bottle I've been saving for a special occasion."

"Well this must be a special occasion, cause this is good stuff."

"I know."

"Well anyway" she said. "You want to know how I got to Kansas City?"

I figured she wanted to tell me so I said, "Sure. What's your story?"

"Would you believe me if I told you I came down here on a riverboat?" she asked.

"Sure. Why not?"

"No kidding."

Turns out there was this guy, William Dixon, who operated an old time steamboat up the Missouri to Bismarck in the spring when the water was high enough. Samantha was a cocktail waitress at a place called "The Peacock" when William Dixon came in. He and Samantha got to talking, had a few drinks, and he asked if she had ever been down south. He asked if she'd like to be a waitress on his boat trip to Saint Louis.

"Wow" I said, "That's pretty cool. So did you do it?"

"Yeah" she said. "I did and for a few nights it was fun. The tips were great, but then he wanted more from me than being a waitress."

William Dixon had wanted to prostitute her to the men on the boat. She refused so when they docked in Kansas City, Dixon took her off the boat. He had a car waiting and she was driven into town and delivered to a pimp that Dixon knew who turned out to be Papa B. She had no idea what Papa had paid Dixon or if Papa had paid Dixon at all. She always assumed he had paid him something, but couldn't prove it, but she'd been with Papa ever since.

She asked for a refill. "Won't you join me?" she asked. "I so hate to drink alone... And this is good whiskey. What did you say this was?"

"I didn't" I answered coldly. I wanted to drink whiskey too. I wanted some really bad. I started battling with myself. Then I started doing the old rationalizing thing. What would it hurt to have one or two after all these years? Surely I could handle it now that I wasn't in the high-pressure situation anymore. I tried hard to talk myself out of it, but for the life of me, I couldn't come up with any reason why I shouldn't have a drink or two with this pretty little lady, this lady who I was rapidly becoming very fond of. She said what she felt. There was nothing fake about this woman. She was young, that was true, but I was definitely attracted to her. I wanted her, and that made me feel slightly guilty. I knew where drinking with this woman might lead, but at that moment, it didn't matter to me.

"OK" I said finally taking her glass. "I'll have one too. We'll talk and get to know each other, Samantha."

I went to the kitchen and poured myself a double. Just straight Jack with ice. I never did see any reason to ruin a good whiskey with a mix, not even water. Just get it good and cold and drink it straight.

Back when I was drinking a lot I used to buy a bottle and put it in the freezer. I'd let it get good and cold, and the drink it straight, no ice. But this whiskey hadn't been in a freezer, so I needed a little ice, frosty as it was. I refreshed Samantha's drink and returned to the living room. I brought the bottle with me and set in on the coffee table.

"Here we are" I said handing her the drink. I took my seat beside her on the couch and we resumed out conversation.

Chapter 9

"I couldn't get it" Hughie said as Max was coming to. Max was still very groggy.   He didn't quite understand what Hughie was trying to tell him. He realized he had a mask of some kind over his nose and mouth. He tired to remove it, but he didn't have the strength.

"'What?" he mumbled, the mask fogging as he spoke. Hughie cranked a knob on a bottle that looked like a small propane tank.

"I gave you Nitrous, Max. Don't take the mask off for a minute." Hughie cranked up the Oxygen feed to the mask. It only took a minute for Max to come around.

"Fuck!" he said, taking the mask from his face. "My arm hurts like hell now."

Hughie twiddled with the valves on the tanks for a minute. He was trying to buy time before he told Max the alarming news. He didn't want to be the one to break it to him but he had no choice.

"I couldn't get the bullet out, Boss." he said.

"What?" Max shouted.

"I tried, but the bone is shattered. The bullet has mushroomed and splattered all over. I can't get it without doing a lot more damage"

Max didn't say anything for a full minute. "You gotta get it outta there, Hughie" he said finally.

"There's no way, Max. Maybe a doctor could get it, but I can't. The bullet mushroomed and is tangled in the bone. Your whole upper arm bone is shattered, Max, with lead all tangled up in there."

"More whiskey, Hughie" Max said his eyes rolling up in his head. Hughie found the bottle, filled Max's glass, and brought it to him. After drinking down half a glass of whiskey, Max asked, "So what do we do?"

Hughie swallowed hard. He took a swig straight from the bottle. "You gotta see a doctor. If you don't, the wound will get infected and then... probably gangrene will set in, and then, you'll lose the arm, Max."

Max frowned and drained his glass. "I can't lose my arm, Hughie" Max answered. "Do you remember the name of that doctor who used to advertise that he'd make house calls?"

Hughie thought hard. He did remember something about a new doctor they'd seen who advertised on local television and billboards around town who claimed to be an old time doctor who made house calls. "I do" he said. "What was his name?"

Max couldn't remember either. "Damn" he said. "Why didn't you pay more attention to the commercials? That's the kind of information I'd think you'd remember."

Hughie was racking his brain. "Doctor... 'S' something. I think his last name started with an 'S'."

"Yeah" Max said. "I think you're right 'Sampson', or "Simpson'. C'mon, Hughie think of it!"

"Sal... Salmon, Salmonson! That's it! Doctor Salmonson."

"Yes!" exclaimed Max. "That's right. Go find him now, Hughie."

Hughie wasted no time. He put on his coat and was about to walk out the door when Max stopped him with a shout. "Hughie!"

Hughie stopped and turned to look at Max.

"Take ten thousand dollars in case this doctor needs a little convincing."

Hughie looked at the duffel bag beside Papa's clothes. "But Max" he protested, "you got shot for that money. Are you sure?"

"Yes! Don't worry about it. Just take ten grand and go find the God damned doctor. Offer him whatever you have to, just get him here!"

Hughie nodded and reached in the bag for the money. He was about to leave again, when suddenly Max shouted for him to bring him Papa's clothes. He wanted to see if there was anything of value in them. Hughie brought Max the clothing and then left saying he would be back with the doctor if he could.

As Max rifled through Papa's pants he found little other than car keys, a wallet with some credit cards, driver's license, and some papers, but no cash. He threw the pants away and began going through the jacket. After searching several pockets and finding some breath mints and a beer bottle cap, he finally found something of value - a cell phone.

"Hmmm." Max hummed. He clicked the send button and reviewed the list of recent calls Papa had received. He scrolled through the list, but didn't recognize any of the names or numbers other than his own. Suddenly he had an idea.

"Let's find out who Papa talked to before he called me" he said aloud to no one but himself. He scrolled to the top of the list. The most recent entry was his own phone number, but a call made earlier was to someone named "Sage Chandler."

"What the hell?" Max thought. He positioned the selector on the stranger's phone number and hit the send button. "Let's just find out who this is." The phone began to ring.

Chapter 10

Just as I was about to take my first drink of whiskey in years, my cell phone went off. It was a call from a dead man. The call was coming from Papa's cell phone. For a second I thought maybe Papa hadn't died at all and was now calling to find out why we had left him there. Then I remembered the severity of his head wounds. He'd been killed alright, no doubt about that. The caller must be the kidnapper. He must have taken Papa's clothes when he retrieved the money, or had someone else retrieve it. The phone must have been in Papa's clothes. I picked up the phone.

"Hello?" I answered.

"Who is this?" the gruff voice on the other end asked.

"Who wants to know?"

"Just tell me who the fuck you are."

I hesitated. I didn't want this kidnapping bastard to know who I was. "I know who you are." I said.

"Do you now?" he asked. "And how the fuck do you know that?"

"Cause you're the one who kidnapped Trixy and shot Papa B."

"Oh so you know about that, huh?" he asked then paused a second. "So you must be the dirty bastard that shot me in the arm."

Now it was my turn to pause a minute. "Yes" I said. "I must be that bastard all right. I'm sorry I missed. You should be dead now."

"Oh you didn't miss. My arm is in bad shape, but not near as bad a shape as you'll be in once I am able to track you down."

I switched the phone to my other hand, grabbed my drink, and took a sip. "Is that a fact?" I asked.

"Oh yeah." he answered. "That is a fact."

I sipped my drink again and considered what my reaction should be. "I've been threatened before, you know" I said. "By big money guys, corporate thugs, mob guys, all kinds of people much more influential than some small time kidnapping rapist like you." Max didn't care for being called a small time kidnapping rapist and he let me know it.

"Listen you smart-ass fucker" he said. "I'm coming to get you. You are going to be dead soon."

"Well, I guess we'll see how it all plays out" I said. I knew from Samantha's story of her kidnapping and watching him kill Papa that this guy was one bad son of bitch. "But you should know that I am usually a better shot than I was tonight."

"Oh you won't get another chance to shoot me, Mr. Chandler." he paused waiting to see how I would respond to his knowing my name. I didn't care for his knowing my name; in fact, he'd managed to rock my confidence a little.

"So you know my name" I said. "Why did you ask who I was then?"

"I wanted to see if I was dealing with an honest man. Evidently, I am not."

I laughed suddenly. It was probably a nervous laugh, but the timing couldn't have been better.

"What the fuck are you laughing at?"

I told him that it just struck me funny that he would say that I am a dishonest man.   Talk about irony, or the pan calling the kettle black or whatever other metaphor fits the situation. "But I don't know your name" I added. "That's hardly fair."

"Yeah" he said in a low voice, "It kind of gives me the advantage doesn't it? Just remember you won't see me coming, Mr. Chandler, just like I didn't see you." And then the phone went dead.

"Damn it!" I said snapping my phone shut. Samantha had inferred who was on the other end of the call. She wanted to know what he had said.

"He knows who you are, doesn't he?"

"The bastard must have Papa's cell phone. Evidently Papa saved my phone number in his phone under my real name."

Samantha looked spooked. "He's a mean fucker, Sage" she said. "We gotta get ready for him."

"Not we" I said. "I've got to get you somewhere safe."

"And where would that be?"

"I didn't know either. "Are there any friends or relatives you could stay with?"

She shook her head rapidly. "Not here. Papa was about the only person I really knew. The only one I could trust."

"Well we've got to get you somewhere." I asked her if she might consider flying home to Bismarck.

"Oh sure, and what would I do there? My parents won't have nothin' to do with me anymore." After a long pause she said, "I've got nowhere else to go, Sage."

I rubbed my temples. I was getting a massive headache. More whiskey I thought and some aspirin.

I stood and walked to the bathroom, found my aspirin bottle and poured three tablets into my hand. Returning to the couch where Samantha still remained seated, I grabbed the whiskey bottle from the coffee table and dumped another few gurgles into my glass. I popped the aspirin and chased them with the booze.

"He said I hit him when I shot him... hit him in the arm he said."

"Good!" said Samantha. "I only wish you'd a killed the bastard." I looked into her eyes and saw hatred. She really wanted this guy dead. I couldn't blame her after what he'd probably done to her.

"Well at least he's laid up for a while" I said. "It buys us some time to make a plan."

"Us?" she questioned. "Did you say us?"

"Yeah us" I replied. She'd said she had nowhere else to go. I couldn't very well just send her out into the night with nowhere to go. I couldn't think of anything else to do with her. She was in this up to her neck, deeper than I really, so what the hell? If she wanted to take a chance on dying with me, who was I to try to stop her?

She looked deep into my eyes and smiled. "My hero" she said. "Let's have one more and then I'll take you to bed and show you how grateful I am." Her idea came as kind of a shock to me. I had been planning to sleep on the couch and let her have my bed. The thought of having sex with this woman had crossed my mind, but I didn't intend to act on it... at least not yet. The only real thoughts I'd had about her were how I would get rid of her before she became a habit.

"No way, mister" she said to my offer of sleeping on the couch. "After what you did for me tonight, you're coming to bed with me."

"Oh Samantha, I am almost twice your age. I don't think it would be right, especially after what you've been through."

"Nonsense" she said, "Most of the men I've been with are older than you are... Besides, I like older men."

This was going to be tough to get out of. I tried acting fatherly. "Now Samantha" I started, "it's not right that we sleep together tonight. We've just met and you have been through a traumatic ordeal."

"Are you married?" she asked.

"Well, no. Not anymore."

"Then what are you so worried about? It's just sex."

"That's not what concerns me."

"Well I'm clean. At least I will be once I have a bath. I don't have aids or any other cooties. And I want to reward your heroic behavior. I want you, Sage. I want you tonight."

"Your cleanliness doesn't worry me either, it's the fact that you're.... so..."

"Its fact that I am a whore that bothers you, isn't it?"

"No" I said more sternly than I mean to. "That's not it either." And it wasn't. I didn't care that she had been a whore. I had long ago lost my high and mighty attitude about people. I realized when I was a drunk that I could have gotten into something just as bad as or worse than prostitution, drugs maybe and selling them to whoever might have enough money to pay for them, even kids.

"I just don't know if it's a good idea for us to sleep together tonight" I said. "I wish I could convince you to go somewhere else. It's not safe for you here."

She looked at me with a kind of hurt on her face. "Its probably not safe for me anywhere" she said. She turned her head away from me.

"What if he does get us? What if he gets us both?" She paused. Was she waiting for me to answer her? What if he did get us? We'd be dead that's what. Rapidly turning to face me again, her eyes burning into mine she said, "I feel safe here with you, Sage, much safer than I'd be anywhere else."

I don't know if it was the whiskey or what, but I was excited, giddy almost, like an adolescent on his first date. I wanted her. There was something about this girl.

We gazed into each other's eyes a moment. She was right. What did I have to lose? My marriage? My job? My self-esteem?

"And he will come" she whispered. "I know he will. He's a real mean bastard, Sage."

I knew he'd come too, at least I felt very strongly that he would. I'd gotten to know these lowlife types over the past few years. Ex-cons, drug addicts, thieves, it's all the same with them. It's all about respect and revenge. He's got the fifty grand, I got shit and *he's* coming after *me*? He should just go somewhere and hide out, but he won't. The criminal mind doesn't work that way. It's all about his reputation and I knew that. If he let someone shoot him without retaliation then every little street punk would think he'd gone soft. So in a show of strength, he'll come and I'll have to kill him, or he'd kill me. Dying didn't frighten me much. What the hell did I have? And the thought of killing a piece of shit like him didn't bother me either. It was true I'd never killed anyone before, but I was pretty certain I wouldn't lose any sleep over shooting this asshole. My biggest problem right now was what the hell to do with Samantha.

We finished our drinks and Samantha stood up and extended her hand. "Come on" she said, "I need a bath. You got a bathtub, don't yah?"

I reached for her hand and let her tug me off the couch and lead me to the bathroom. I knew better, but I couldn't help myself. Maybe it was the whiskey or maybe it was just her. She was a good-looking hottie with a smoking hot body, even in that drab, loose-fitting dress she wore. I was but a man and it had been quite a while since I'd been with a woman. I let her lead and I just went along for the ride.

She led me to the bathroom and told me to sit on the toilet. She sat on the edge of the bathtub and began to draw a bath. After she had adjusted the water to suit herself, she stood, unzipped her dress and let it fall to the floor. She was so uninhibited. I had never met anyone so comfortable with her own body. She was completely naked after taking off the dress. Its was the only clothing she wore. She got in the tub.

"Burn that dress, will yah?" she asked.

"Its pretty ugly" agreed, "but I don't know if it deserves burning. It's all the clothing you have at the moment."

She smiled and lay back in the tub totally immersing herself. I put my hand in the water, and pulled it right out again. It was way too hot for me. How could she stand it?

"Want to join me?" she asked.

"Yes" I said, "but I can't take water that hot." She laughed and submerged her head underwater. She blew a few bubbles and came up laughing.

"If you can't stand the heat" she said, "get out of the bathroom." She laughed again. Her laugh turned me on. She was so beautiful. I wanted nothing more than to get in that tub with her and I told her so. She reached up with her right foot and turned on the cold water faucet.

"Come on in, then" she said. "I'll cool it off for you."

I stripped and got in the tub. Even with the added cold water, it was still pretty hot. Eventually I became accustomed to it. I sat with her feet next to me, caressing them. My bathtub wasn't really big enough for two but we made do. I found the hot water relaxing and invigorating at the same time. The hot water was melting away the muscle tension of the day, but being with her naked in the tub was causing stiffness in another area.

When we'd had enough, we drained the tub and showered off. We left the bathroom wrapped in towels. I was physically drained. My legs would barely hold me up let alone propel me forward. We went to bed and crashed. I knew she wanted to make love, but we were both exhausted and the bath had drained any ambition we'd had left. We slept peacefully, cuddled and entwined in each other's arms. After getting a few hours sleep, we woke up and made sweet love for a solid hour. It was marvelous. Then we went back to sleep until late afternoon.

Chapter 11

Three hours after he'd gone in search of a doctor, Hughie returned empty handed. "I can't find a doctor who will come, Boss" he said. "I looked everywhere I and called everyone I knew who might know someone, but nothing."

Max didn't answer. He just stared blankly at Hughie.

"Just let me take you to the hospital, Max. There's no other way."

"Who the hell did you call that might know someone?" Max asked. "I told you which doctor to go to... what happened to him?"

Hughie explained that this doctor had gotten so much public reaction to his house call campaign that he had all the patients he could handle. "He's not seeing any new patients."

"Not seeing new patients?" Max blared. "Did you offer him the ten grand?"

Hughie had offered him the money, but the doctor said he wasn't motivated by money anymore, especially if there was a chance it was dirty money. "He doesn't need guys like us anymore, I guess."

Max stood up from the couch and almost fell back down again. "You've lost a lot of blood already, Boss" said Hughie. "Don't try to do too much too fast."

"Ah fuck you, Hughie" Max said. "If you were worth a shit, you could'a found me a doctor. God damn it, now I gotta go to a hospital with a gunshot wound. You know what that means, Hughie?"

Hughie didn't answer. He just stood there with a stupid look on his face, but he knew well enough what Max was driving at: that hospitals report gunshot wounds to the authorities.

"I haven't seen my P.O. in three months. You know the cops are looking for me." Hughie knew damn well the incident Max was referring to.

A couple months ago, Max and Hughie had crossed the river to the Kansas side of town looking for some action. They drove around for a while and checked out some street hookers, but they didn't see anything they liked well enough to pay for. Max was a very bigoted man. There was no way he was going to pay for sex with a black girl.

They finally gave up on their prostitute search and stopped at a bar. They got to drinking pretty heavy and bar hopping. After they'd had quite a few they wound up in a little bar called Mike's Place. It was a small bar with two pool tables and a jukebox. There wasn't enough room for live music, which was fine with Max. He didn't care much for music anyway.

A man came in and began spending a lot of money, buying round and after round for the house. Max figured if the guy wanted to throw his money away, he should throw some his way.

"Better he gives it to us, than to the bartender" Max had said to Hughie before they began making plans.

They finished their beers and left the bar. Max made a big deal about leaving, saying goodbye to everyone and thanking the man who'd bought all the drinks. He wanted everyone to see him leave, but he and Hughie didn't leave. Instead they waited for the man outside the bar. When he finally came out, Max grabbed him and hauled him around the corner of the bar. Then he hit him so hard he knocked him out with one blow. Even though the man was out cold, Max continued to beat hell out of him for no other reason than pure enjoyment. He kept kicking him in the ribs, and the face. He stomped on his hand with the heel of his boot, twice. Hughie tried to get Max to stop, but he wouldn't. When Max gets that way, there's no stopping him.

When Max finally finished beating the daylights out of the poor fellow, he rifled through the man's pockets and found his money. Even after all the money the man had spent in the bar, Max took almost five thousand dollars off him. Then he noticed his watch. It wasn't a Rolex, but Max figured it was worth a grand at least.

The next day the Star reported the incident. The man Max robbed was in a hospital in critical condition with a broken collarbone, broken ribs, bruised lungs, and a demolished right hand. His face was so badly beaten he was hardly recognizable. Both eyes were swollen shut, his nose was broken in three places, he'd lost his two front teeth and his left cheekbone was shattered. Doctors feared the damage caused to the left eye could render him blind in that eye. Only time would tell. After the swelling went down they'd be better able to make a determination.

The account also gave an accurate description of Max but not Hughie which was understandable. Max was a huge man standing almost six feet, seven inches tall and weighed well over two hundred and fifty pounds. He stood out in a crowd. Hughie on the other hand was a very average looking man. No outstanding features. Hughie was five feet, ten inches tall, with an average build and average features. He was unremarkable in every way, and therefore, forgettable, a trait that had served Hughie well on more than that one occasion.

A few days later, the cops came by the house where Hughie and Max were living to talk to Max. They wanted to question him about the incident since he'd been identified by two witnesses who'd seen him in the bar that night. He wasn't a suspect, but he had been recognized by people at the bar. The cops just wanted to ask if he'd seen anyone who might have perpetrated the crime. Max wasn't home, however, so the cops left saying they'd be back later. When Max returned he should call the number on the card they'd left with Hughie.

When Max did come home, Hughie related the story of the cops' visit. Max decided then and there he and Hughie would have to move. He knew of a place in an abandoned part of town where they could lay low. It wasn't the Hilton, but it would do for a while until they could make one big score and leave Kansas City altogether. He and Hughie had been hiding out in the West Bottoms ever since living off the five G's, Max had taken off the man at the bar. But now their money was running out. So they decided to kidnap a high dollar hooker and hold her for ransom. The plan had worked perfectly except for Max being shot.

"Alright" Max said, "Take me to the hospital and I'll take my chances with the law."

"Good call Max" Hughie said. "Even if they do inform the cops that you are in the hospital, they ain't got no evidence anyway. Nobody saw us that night. They got shit."

"You better hope they got shit, Hughie, cause if I go down, you go down."

They left the abandoned house they had been living in for the past three months. Hughie helped Max into the car and drove him to the Shawnee Mission Medical Center; the hospital which Hughie figured was the closest. Hughie drove to the emergency door, parked and helped Max out of the car. A nurse came out with a wheelchair and Max was happy to sit down. The nurse wheeled him off to the emergency room. "I'll be right here, Boss," Hughie shouted. "Its gonna be alright."

Hughie moved his car to the parking lot. He was able to find a parking place close to the emergency room. There weren't many cars parked at the hospital that time of night.

He entered the emergency room and was told Max had been moved into 'ER' and he couldn't see him right then. But there was a waiting room down the hall with coffee and donuts. He should wait there until Max is out of ER and assigned to a room.

Hughie didn't want to sit in a waiting room, drinking stale coffee and reading old magazines. He figured Max was in good hands and probably wouldn't miss him if he slipped out, so he left the hospital and began driving back to the shitty little hovel in the West Bottoms.

He thought as he drove about what he'd be doing now if he'd let the scalpel cut Max's throat. He'd be rid of Max once and for all and maybe then he could get his life back on track. He knew if he kept hanging out with Max that'd he wind up back in prison, or worse, but he knew he couldn't just walk out on Maxwell Brown. If the relationship was to be ended, Max would insist on being the one who ended it, and Hughie had seen firsthand what that meant.

Now would be a good time to leave, but he didn't have the money to go anywhere. He could take the fifty thousand Max took off the pimp, but Hughie knew he didn't have the guts for that. He figured that if he did that, Max would find him no matter where he went, even if he left the country, Max would find him somehow, someday, and that would be the end.

No, it was better to hang on now. Damn! Why hadn't he simply cut Max's arteries when he'd had the chance. Max would be dead now, and Hughie would have the fifty thou to himself. He could simply drive away and go wherever he wished. Hughie was ashamed of himself for not having the courage to just finish it.

He drove along kicking himself until he finally reached the rats nest in the West Bottoms he had come to call home. He got out of the car and entered the house. He suddenly got the feeling that this was all going to end badly for him. He could go to the cops and turn himself in. He could cut a deal with them. Maybe if Hughie testified in court that Max had beaten and mugged that man at Mikes Place, maybe they'd cut a deal and Hughie would get off. No. That was no good. The cops might not deal, and even if they did, Max had too many connections in prison. They'd find Hughie even if he left the country. Nope. Too risky. The only thing to do now was hide the money and guns somewhere and ride it out. The only decision Hughie had to make was where to hide the money and guns where the cops wouldn't find them.

Chapter 12

I awoke about 3:30 in the afternoon. Samantha was already up. It had been quite a morning. I hadn't enjoyed myself so much in a good many years. I lay there a while enjoying the memories of the beautiful time we'd had together. It reminded me of when Kim and I were first married.

We'd been so much in love and the first few years before the kids came and everything got so crazy. Would Samantha stick around? Did I want her to? At that moment, I hoped she would. On the other hand, I was at least twenty years older than she was. For all I knew, I was older than her father. How could we bridge the inevitable generation gap between us?

I got up, stretched and searched my dresser for my favorite sweats and my old Led Zeppelin T-shirt I'd had since... Since when? God it seemed like I'd had that shirt forever and it looked like it too all full of holes the way it was. "It might be older than Samantha" I thought. Generation gap number one?

Once I dressed I left the bedroom to find Samantha in the kitchen busily cooking breakfast. When she heard me approaching, she gestured for me to come to her. She was wearing one of my long-sleeve dress shirts she'd gotten out of my closet and nothing else. She'd rolled the sleeves a little way up her arms. God she looked good in that shirt. I sneaked up behind her and wrapped my arms around her waist.

"Hungry?" she asked smiling as she turned in my arms.

"Starving" I answered kissing her gently.

"Well" she said, "you didn't have much in your fridge, but I've got bacon and scrambled eggs with cheese and some fried potatoes."

"Sounds delicious" I said walking toward the cabinet, taking down a cup and filling it with fresh coffee. "Coffee smells good too," I said.

I sat down at the kitchen table and watched her cook. I sipped my coffee and noticed a slight headache from the whiskey. "How do you feel today?" I asked,

"I feel pretty good, actually" she answered. "You?"

"Got a slight headache from the whiskey, but other than that, pretty good too."

"Well you'll feel better after you eat something." She set a plate in front of me "Dig in."

"I'll wait for you."

"Nonsense. Dig in."

I tasted the eggs first. "Man" I said, "what did you season these eggs with?"

"Tut, tut" she said bringing her plate to the table. "Family secret. Can't tell you."

Whatever she had used, she used just the right amount. They were the best scrambled eggs I'd had in a long time.

Same with the bacon and potatoes. "You're a mighty fine cook" I told her. "I didn't know I had seasoning in the house that tasted like this."

"I worked summers as a short order cook in a little cafe in Bismarck during high school."

"Well they taught you well."

We hungrily ate our breakfasts without much conversation. She was as hungry as I was. I realized it might have been some time since she'd eaten anything of substance.

"Did he feed you while he held you captive?" I asked.

"Yeah" she answered, "some shit from a can, you know stew, chili, peaches, and some bread. I think it was the drugs, but I didn't feel like eating most of the time."

"What drugs?" I asked. "You're not into drugs, are you?"

"No" she said as if I'd insulted her. "That guy... the kidnapper dude, he gave me some kind of drugs that made me... not hungry."

That made me feel better. There for a second, I thought my dream would be shattered because she was a junkie or something.

After breakfast, we washed the dishes together. She washed, I dried, and we retired to the living room with our coffee. We chatted for a while about little things like what kind of food we like, favorite television shows, music, and finally realized we had a lot in common. We both liked the old music, rock and country. I told her I kind of liked Frank Sinatra, to which she answered, "Who?" That was the second sign of the generation gap that I hoped wouldn't turn into a generation ravine.

I explained who Frank Sinatra was, told her about Dino, Sammy and the Rat Pack. She laughed heartily at that word, "Rat Pack." She thought that was funny for some reason. I couldn't believe she'd never heard of any of these people.

Finally Samantha asked, "So what are we going to do if that bastard shows up?"

"We're gonna try not to get killed" I answered. "I don't really want to kill anyone either, but when I think about what that son of a bitch did to you... How can people treat other people that way?"

"I know" she said, "I hope you do kill that fucking bastard. I hate him more than you can imagine. In fact, I'll kill him myself if you'll let me have a gun. I'll shoot him on sight."

"Can you handle a gun?" I asked.

"Oh hell yes! My dad made sure I knew how to shoot in case times got tough and I had to actually hunt for food someday."

She pulled her legs up underneath her sitting sideways as women sometimes do. "I am deadly with a rifle, shotgun or pistol."

"Automatic or revolver?"

"Either. I used to clean all the weapons after Dad and I came back from target practice. I can field strip and clean a Glock blindfolded."

"Can you now?"

"Damn right I can... Why, you got one?"

"As a matter of fact, I do. Two of 'em. A forty and a forty five."

"Ooo," she said almost jumping off the couch. "Can I see them?"

I got up and walked to the bedroom and returned with my .40. I dumped the mag into my left hand and handed her the gun.

"Don't trust me, huh?" she said smiling.

"I just didn't want it to be loaded."

Almost before I had gotten the words out she had removed the slide, barrel, and spring and laid them on the coffee table before her. She picked up the barrel and looked down it holding her thumbnail at the other end to reflect the light into the barrel.

"Clean" she said. "I'm impressed."

"You're impressed?" I said emphatically. "I've never stripped that gun that fast in my life. I usually have trouble getting the slide off.

"Yeah" she answered, "There's a trick to it. I'll show you some time."

She handed me the barrel, picked up the receiver and examined it pulling the trigger and watching the mechanisms at work.

"Got a little gunk in here, hon" she said. "Get your cleaning kit and I'll fix it up for ya."

What kind of hooker knows this much about automatic weapons I wondered as I went to retrieve the kit.

"OK" I said, handing her the cleaning kit. "What gives? Why do you know so much about guns?"

"I told you. I'm a country girl. My dad wanted to make sure I knew how to fend for myself so he taught me about guns."

"God damn" I said, "you can cook, you know weapons and I know how good you are in the sack... What other secrets do you have?"

"Oh not many" she said as she used the cleaning brush on the receiver. "Well, maybe one or two, but you'll have to wait. A girl can't reveal too much about herself all at once."

I hoped she wasn't referring to some deep-seated psychological condition like being molested as a child by Uncle Clem or something. I was really starting to fall for this girl.

I sat on the couch beside her and watched her as she diligently cleaned the weapon. She seemed to be absorbed in cleaning the gun. I wanted to ask if she felt the way I did. I didn't know if it was the right time or not. I hesitated for an instant, then blurted "So..." but I didn't finish. She immediately stopped cleaning and turned to look at me with a questioning look.

"Yes?" she questioned.

"I think we might have something starting here, do you?" I felt like a teenager asking her to go steady with me.

"You and me?" she asked going back to her cleaning.

"Yeah you and me."

"Well... Yes... I do, Sage."

"So tell me then. Are there other skeletons in your closet I should know about?"

She carefully set the receiver on the coffee table and sat back almost to a lying position. She looked at me briefly, took a deep breath and said, "OK. I'll tell you."

Samantha said she was raised in Bismarck, North Dakota. She attended elementary and high school there and did work at a little cafe during the summers after her Junior and Senior years. But then the story changed somewhat from the one she'd told me the night before.

It turns out she went to the University of North Dakota in Fargo after high school. She dropped out after her sophomore year, however, to marry a man named Kevin Roland. They were married for two years, before they found out Kevin couldn't father children. "His fish weren't swimming" as Samantha put it. Plus, he was lazy and refused to get a real job. He thought of himself as a professional musician even though he played only occasionally on weekends.

Samantha tried to make the marriage work. She even suggested they adopt a child, but Kevin shot that down too. He couldn't bring a child into their house until he made the big time music scene, but he wasn't willing to move to a music town like L.A., Nashville, or Austin. He somehow thought he'd make it hanging around eastern North Dakota and Minnesota.

Finally they divorced. Samantha wanted to use the same lawyer so they could divorce as inexpensively as possible, but Kevin had other plans. He found his own attorney and Samantha wound up paying him alimony.

She'd wanted to return to college, but thought she needed to gather some money first.

"That was a huge mistake" she said. "I should have just went back to school even if I had to get loans to do it." But she hadn't. Rather, she'd gone to work as a waitress in a truck stop cafe and had gotten by as best as she could.

She couldn't afford to live and pay alimony on her meager salary as a waitress, so a friend told her about a strip club where she could dance and make three or four times as much as she could as a waitress. She began dancing at the little club one or two nights a week. She was one of the most popular dancers and the tips were fabulous. After a while she became the top-draw dancer. She was bringing home five hundred or more a night. She loved the money, but she felt guilty about dancing naked for a bunch of horny truck drivers.

When the riverboat man, William Dixon, came into the club and offered her a job as a waitress on his riverboat, promising a good salary and great tips, she decided to go for it. It wouldn't pay as well as dancing, but at least she wouldn't be ashamed of it.

Another plus was she'd be away from Fargo.

"Kevin was calling and coming around" she said. "He actually wanted to get back together. He said he'd 'rethought' the adoption idea."

Samantha thought that if she left on the riverboat she could get away from paying Alimony. Maybe she' find a new place; a new life. "I was young, Sage" she said. "I thought running away was the answer."

Everything went fine, just like Dixon said, but one night the riverboat man came and asked her to pleasure an especially affluent male passenger for money. He promised her it would be the only time and she'd be rewarded financially. She refused and that didn't sit well with Dixon, but he didn't nag her about it, at least not for a while.

A week later, Dixon came around again offering her good money to have sex with another passenger. She again refused.

"I told Dixon" she said, "that I am not a prostitute no matter how much he wanted me to be." Dixon reminded her that he had found her in a strip club taking off her clothes for money and that most strippers he'd ever known would perform sexual favors for money.

"Not me" she said angrily. "I never did that. I was only a dancer."

"Then dance here" Dixon demanded. "No sex, just dancing."

She knew that if she started dancing it would just be the first step in her transition to prostitute, but she told herself, the money would be good. She also knew that her relationship with Mr. Dixon was about to end, so she agreed to dance, but dancing was as far as she was willing to go. She planned to jump ship at the next opportunity.

For two weeks she danced in the ship's gentleman's club in addition to her regular cocktail waitress job. When Dixon came around again asking her to "sex up" a passenger she told him to go to hell; that she'd be off the boat at the very next stop but Dixon beat her to the punch.

When the boat stopped in Kansas City, Dixon and two of his hired helpers hauled her downtown to meet Papa B. She was forced to dance for Papa and he liked what he saw. Dixon sold her to Papa for some amount. She never did know what Papa had paid for her, but she'd never felt so used in her life. "He just sold me, Sage" She said, "like a used car, and Papa paid for me like he was buying a pet."

Papa kept such close tabs on her, there was no way she could escape. She tried a few times, but found that Papa's wrath was severe. The punishment she'd suffer with each escape and recapture became more brutal until it just wasn't worth it anymore.

She finally came to accept her fate. "Life became much easier when I stopped fighting it" She said. Papa supplied her with everything she wanted and all the drugs she desired. At first she used to stay high all the time on cocaine and pills because she couldn't stand what she had been forced to become. It was easier to do what she had to do if she was buzzed up on coke most of the time.

The problem was that the drugs were making her lazy. She wasn't working out or eating right and was becoming flabby. Finally Papa mentioned that the big spenders don't like flabby women and that if she didn't get back in shape he wouldn't be able to ensure her the best Johns anymore. Besides she had begun to worry that she was burning her nose out with her constant cocaine snorting. She decided to give up the drugs and just do it straight. "It was tough at first" she said. "I had a pretty bad coke habit." She became accustomed to working without coke eventually. She told herself it was just a job no different from any other, but paid much better. "Besides" she said, "I liked sex as long as it was just straight sex. So actually I had a pretty good job."

She sold herself on the idea as hard as she could and for a while believed it. Sex was nothing to be ashamed of. Everyone did it. It just happened that she got paid for it, but that was no crime, not really.

Eventually she even started having fond feelings for Papa. As long as she did what she was told, they got along fine. He provided a fine place for her to live. There was always plenty of good food; she had her own exercise room with treadmills, nautilus machines, and free weights. There was a pool where she could swim, a hot tub to relax after her workouts. As long as she stayed fit, Papa set her up with the richest and safest of his customers. She was with him for about two years.

"That's the truth, Sage" she said with a sort of pitiful look that pulled at my heartstrings. "Now all I want is get away from that life; to find someone who I love and who will love me." She let me contemplate her story for a moment before saying, "Do you believe me?"

I wanted to believe her. I needed to believe her. Why wouldn't I believe her? Her story sounded plausible to me. Look at the wreck I'd made of my life, and I wasn't dragged into slavery, "Yes I believe you, honey" I said, "Of course I believe you."

"Good" she said with a huge smile. She held out her arms to me and I pulled her close to me. We hugged and kissed for a few minutes.

"Now" she said, "as long as we're coming clean, I think there is more to your life than you've told me, so... What's your story?"

She had such a pretty smile. Papa must have had a good dental plan too, because she had almost perfect teeth, covered most of the time by full lips, unless she was smiling. When she smiled, her lips thinned slightly and wrinkled just a bit at the corners of her mouth to display her beautiful, white teeth.

"Alright" I said, "that's only fair, but maybe we should have some more of that good whiskey while I tell you."

I knew I was playing with fire. Both the whiskey and this woman were dangerous commodities, but I had become so enamored with her, I just couldn't help myself. I told myself I could handle the whiskey. As long as I didn't drink every day, I'd be fine. Of course I denied the fact that if I drank today, that would be two days in a row already.

I went to the kitchen and poured two short glasses and returned to the living room. I handed her one of the glasses, sat down beside her, and began to tell her my whole, sad story after law school. She seemed astonished that I had been a lawyer, especially an upscale, corporate lawyer. She was even further surprised that I had given it all up. I assured her it was true, but still I had to show her my diploma before she believed I wasn't kidding.

"Here it is" I said, "The degree of 'Juris Doctor', from the University of Montana."

"You went to law school in Montana?" she asked. She seemed impressed.

"Yeah" I said. "I'm a Montana boy." I explained that my father had been a Lawyer in Missoula and that I had grown up in a little town south of Missoula called Stevensville. She had no idea where that was, but said she had considered attending MSU before deciding on Fargo.

"I know where Bozeman is" she said, "but where is Stevensville?" I knew I had a map of Montana somewhere. I went to see if I could find it. While I looked she held my diploma a while and marveled over it.

"I wish I'd stayed in school" she said. "If I had one of these, I'd frame it and hang it on the wall."

"Mine used to hang on a wall in my office" I said still hunting for the map, "but now it just doesn't seem to mean that much."

I returned with the map and sat beside Samantha. We spread the map before us on the coffee table and I pointed out Missoula, Stevensville, and the Bitterroot range.

"Those are my favorite mountains in Montana" I said.

"I bet they're beautiful. Will you take me there someday?" I was delighted at the idea that she was talking about our future. I wasn't sure that making a life with a mid-twenties ex prostitute was at all practical, but I wanted to believe it was. I let the romantic in me take the wheel and I just went along for the ride. I was enjoying her company and enjoying myself more than I had in a very long time. I didn't want it to end.

Samantha and I just hung out for the rest of the day. We cuddled on the couch and watched a movie on television. I told her about my childhood. I told her about how my father and I used to go hunting every fall up in the Bitterroot range. "We seldom ever shot anything" I said, "but we had a lot of fun hanging out together."

My father and I weren't big time hunters who camped out and stayed until we filled our tags. We'd just go up into the mountains every Sunday during hunting season and drive around until we found a likely spot. My mother would pack a lunch for us and we'd sit in the pickup and eat our sandwiches and drink coffee from a thermos.

We'd leave our sandwiches on the dashboard still wrapped in the plastic wrap my mother had put them in and go look around for some deer. When we returned for lunch, the cheese on the sandwiches would be slightly melted and we'd be starving from the morning's hike. There's nothing better than a bologna and cheese sandwich, heated by the sun, and coffee with your father when you are twelve or thirteen years old.

Another thing my father and I did every spring in early May I think it was, we'd float the Smith River. "Now that was a trip."

We packed up our raft and fishing gear and all our provisions and head for White Sulfur Springs where we'd stay the night and then early in the morning, we'd put in and float all day. Sometimes we fished, sometimes we'd just lay back and let the current take us. Except when we'd hit whitewater. Then we'd have to use our oars to steer and navigate down the river.

"Where is White Sulfur Springs?" Samantha asked.

I pointed it out on the map and she traced the Smith River with her finger.

We talked some more, ate a light supper and went to bed early. We both slept well and were up early the next morning. As I came out of the bedroom yawning, Samantha was in the kitchen cooking breakfast. Again she was wearing the same long-sleeved dress shirt she'd had on the day before. I was in my Led Zeppelin T-shirt and favorite sweats just as I had been the day before. The only difference was this morning I was enjoying my coffee while reading the newspaper.

"Not much news" I said out loud to no one in particular. "There was been a fire downtown near the Plaza yesterday afternoon. No one was killed, two people injured."

I thumbed through a few more pages scanning a few articles when finally and suddenly a headline grabbed my attention:

MURDER IN THE WEST BOTTOMS

A BODY WAS FOUND IN FRONT OF THE
CRANE CO. BUILDING IN THE WEST
BOTTOMS YESTERDAY. THE VICTIM WAS
DESCRIBED AS A BLACK MALE BETWEEN
THE AGES OF 45 AND 50. HE WAS FOUND
NAKED ON THE SIDEWALK, AN APPARENT
VICTIM OF AN ASSASSINATION. POLICE
SUSPECT GANG ACTIVITY. OTHER DETAILS
ARE BEING WITHHELD UNTIL A POSITIVE
IDENTIFICATION CAN BE MADE AND NEXT
OF KIN NOTIFIED.

That was it. A short little blurb on page 5 of the Kansas
City Star. It's sad how little affect murder has on the media
these days, I thought.

"Here it is" I said.

"Here what is?" asked Samantha.

"They found Papa."

"Oh Jeez. Let me see."

I handed her the paper as she sat down beside me. She
read the blurb and teared up a little. "Poor Papa" she said.
"I'll miss him."

'Who do you suppose they'll get to ID him?" I asked.

"Luckily, "they don't know where I am. Otherwise they'd
probably pick me for it."

"Why you?"

"Oh the cops know me and my affiliation with Papa." She
looked up from the paper directly into my eyes. With a slight
smile she said, "I've been in the jug a time or two, Sage."

Our eyes remained locked for a few moments. "I don't care" I said absently. "Anyway, maybe you should volunteer to ID the body."

"What? Why would I want to do that?"

"Well you could look through the photo book for possible suspects. Maybe you'd recognize the killer if you saw a picture."

"Maybe" she said doubtfully, "but I bet the cops already know who Papa is. He was no stranger to the cops in this town. He was always bailing one of us girls out of jail."

I pondered that thought for a while. It was true sometimes the police did withhold information from the press during an on-going investigation. They usually blamed waiting on a positive ID, but many times they already had the victim's name.

"Well" I said, "you might be right about that, but still I think we should see if you can pick the guy out of the mug shot book."

She looked sheepish but before she could protest I said, "We'd be in much better shape if we knew who this bastard was. As it is now, he knows my name, but we don't know his."

"I guess," she said reluctantly, "Its worth a try I suppose."

"One thing, though" I said, "We'll have to come clean with the cops and tell them what you were doing before being kidnapped."

"Oh, I don't care about that" she said. "I'll probably know the cop anyway, but..."

"What?" I asked.

"I can't very well go down there dressed in just your shirt."

I laughed. "No, I guess you can't."

Chapter 13

Max was lying in his hospital bed wondering if the hospital authorities had notified the cops that they had admitted a gunshot victim last night when a knock came at the door. A man dressed in a lab coat entered and introduced himself as the doctor who had removed the bullet. He'd just come by to deliver his diagnosis.

"We lucked out" the doctor said. "The bullet was lodged in the humerus and had not only fractured the bone, but splintered it." Seeing that, the doctor said he'd become very worried, but once he'd gotten the bullet out, he was able to wrap a sheet of surgical steel around the splintered bone and fasten it with screws.

"The screws will probably remain there for the rest of your life" the doctor said. "However, the screws will sometimes work themselves loose."

"What happens if they do?" Max asked.

"Then a surgeon will have to go in and remove them, but the bone will be completely healed by then."

The doctor went on to explain that sometimes, rarely, but sometimes, the body will reject the foreign material and an infection can start. In that case the surgical steel and screws would have to be removed immediately. Also, even more rarely, some people are allergic to the surgical steel. Again, the hardware would have to come out immediately.

"But so far" the doctor said, "you seem to be doing just fine. I am certain the procedure will be a complete success. Just the same though, I would like to keep you here a couple of days for observation."

"Fine by me, Doc" Max said. He felt like he could certainly use the rest. He felt tired, exhausted almost. He was in no hurry to get up and move around. He'd just lie there and sleep, watch a little television and take it easy.

The next morning however when the nurse brought his breakfast, she informed him that taking it easy wasn't in the cards.

"I'll be back a little later" she said, "to take you for a short walk." Max protested. He wasn't interested in walking, but the nurse insisted that he needed to get up and around to help healing and avoid fluid getting into his lungs.

"Besides" she added, "wouldn't you like to get rid of that catheter?"

"Yeah" Max said, "I meant to ask you about that. Why the catheter?"

"Standard equipment for all surgical procedures, but as soon as you are up and around and able to use the bathroom yourself, I'll remove it."

The nurse left and Max ate his breakfast. The food wasn't bad for hospital food, but it wasn't great either. Hughie's cooking was usually pretty bad, so Max's palette was not accustomed to gourmet food. He felt like a poor judge of the quality of the hospital's food.

When the nurse returned to get Max up and around, she started by asking him to sit on the edge of the bed.

"Don't go too fast" she said. "Sometimes the anesthesia can leave you a bit woozy." Plus Max hadn't exactly been light on the self-dosing morphine pump either. The first night in this bed found him pushing the button pretty much continuously. He'd push the button, sleep for what seemed like ten or fifteen minutes, wake up with his arm throbbing, and push the button again. Sometimes he'd get some morphine, sometimes he wouldn't.

Max sat up and kicked his legs over the edge of the bed. He sat there momentarily and as the nurse had predicted, he felt lightheaded and a bit nauseous.

"Just sit still a minute" the nurse said. "The dizziness should pass in a minute or so."

In a little while, he did feel better. "Are you ready to stand?" the nurse asked.

"No, but you're not going to give me a choice, are you?" The nurse just smiled. Max nodded and the nurse grabbed his good arm and heaved trying to help him as much as possible. He finally stood erect and towered over the nurse by a good ten inches. He tried to walk but the nurse stopped him.

"Don't try to go anywhere yet" she said. "Your catheter bottle is still connected to the side of the bed."

Max looked down and saw what she meant. She asked how he felt. Did he feel strong enough to make it to the bathroom? Max looked at the bathroom. It was only about 10 feet away, but for some reason looked much farther.

"I think so" he said.

She knelt down and unconnected the bottle from the bedside and connected it to his portable IV cart. With little assistance from her, he walked to the bathroom door and back to the bed.

"That's enough for today" she said, "but I think we can pull that catheter if you want to."

Max flinched at the thought. He vaguely remembered how it felt going in. He wasn't sure how it would feel coming out, but the thought made him uneasy. He sat on the edge of the bed and the nurse helped him swing his legs up. He lay down and she covered him. She reached under his blankets, got hold of the catheter and just like that, she removed it. No pain at all. He felt a slight squirt of piss accompany the catheter's departure, but other than that, it was pretty painless and not at all embarrassing.

"Does that feel better?" she asked.

"Much better, Nurse, thank you."

Max was relieved to be free of that damn thing. Being tethered to your bed by your penis is not a comforting feeling. Now he was free to move around. He still had to take the IV cart with him, but other than that one tube running fluids and antibiotics into his arm, he was unencumbered.

Later that same day, A detective named Jack Marble came to visit Max. The detective knocked on the hospital room door, and entered after Max had invited him in. He was tall, not as tall as Max, maybe a bit over six feet, and slim. Dark hair, mid-forties. He wore a dark suit. Max couldn't decide if it was dark blue or black, but either way, he looked like a plain clothes Dick.

"So you found me" Max said after Marble flashed his badge.

"Yup" Marble said. "Sooner or later we always find 'em. I don't know if you're aware, but we've been looking for you for a while now. Where you been keeping yourself?"

"In a hospital room currently."

"Well yeah I gathered that, but where have you been the past three months or so?"

"Around" answered Max, "you know, here and there."

"We surveilled the house on Maple where you were living, but you never came home, Max."

"I've been busy."

"And now you finally took a bullet, huh?"

"What do you want, cop?"

Marble walked to the foot of the bed and stared down at Max and pretended to inspect the bed. Max had no idea why but he suspected Marble was building suspense through silence and diversion.

"How's the arm feeling, Max" he asked.

"Fine!" he said sharply. "Never felt better. What do you want? State your business."

Marble explained that Max had originally been wanted by the police for simple routine questioning. He'd been seen at Mike's Place the night of the assault and robbery. "We have two eye witnesses who've identified you from the mug book. To begin with, we thought you might be a possible witness" Marble said.

"What about now? Am I a suspect now?"

"More like a person of interest."

Marble said that when Max was up and around again, he'd be back to take him in for questioning.

"That is unless you have something to tell me now."

"I don't even know what you're talking about."

"C'mon, Max. Don't play stupid with me. Its beneath you."

Max glared at him for a moment, trying to stare a hole in him with his mind.

"No. Seriously" Max said. "I don't know what you are talking about."

Marble studied him a while trying to find a sign that Max was lying. He came around the side of the bed and kicked it.

"You mean you didn't hear about the man who was beaten half to death outside a little bar over on the Kansas side?"

"No" Max said. "What happened?"

Marble nodded his head and moved back toward the door. "What about the murder in the West Bottoms the other night Max? Did you hear about that?" Marble was watching Max's body language closely. There was nothing detectable in Max's physical reaction to indicate he was lying.

"Murder" Max mumbled. "What murder?"

Marble didn't answer. He was still studying Max's body language, but Max just lay there glaring at Marble.

"C'mon, man" Max said finally. "If you want to ask me questions, come back and get me after I am released, but right now I'm kind of tired."

"OK... alright, that's fair." Marble paused, but didn't seem to be leaving. "But first... who shot you, Max?"

"Nobody" Max replied, "Its a self-inflicted wound. I shot myself when I was cleaning my gun."

Marble laughed heartily. "That's the oldest story in the book, Max." Marble continued laughing. Max thought it was a fake laugh but had to admit, Marble was pretty good at it.

"You shouldn't even have a gun, Max. You're on parole. Does your P.O. know you have a gun?"

"Yeah. He knows I have a gun. He helped me buy it in fact."

Marble frowned at that statement. "Well, I doubt that" he said. "I know you're parole officer and *she* is a nice lady. I'm sure she'd be interested in your being in possession of a gun."

"She?" Max actually looked surprised for a second. "Whatever. Last I checked my Parole Officer's name was Hornigar, and he was definitely a man."

"Things change, Max. Hornigar retired three months ago. You'd know that if you were reporting regularly."

"Is that all, Detective? Are you finished? I need to get my rest."

"Yeah, Max, that's all for now. I'll be back with your new P.O. to get you in a few days when they release you from this place. Don't call anyone for a ride. We will come to get you."

Marble turned on his heel like a soldier and walked toward the door. Without saying anything more he left the room. Max was fuming inside. He was so pissed off he wanted to rip Marble's throat out.

"He thinks he's so fucking special" Max said to himself. "I'll get a that son of a bitch too when this is all over."

Max lay there contemplating what the cops could have on him. Were there witnesses outside the bar that he hadn't seen? He had recognized a couple guys in the bar that night and he'd made such a commotion leaving, he wasn't at all surprised that he was recognized. He'd wanted to be recognized. He'd wanted to be seen leaving early, long before Mr. Moneybags left. That way, all witnesses would be able to say was they'd seen Max and another man in the bar enjoying a few beers and then they left.

Max had been in this position before. He figured the cops would try to intimidate him with their typical cop methods, but it won't work. It never worked. Max had never squealed on anyone, especially himself.

"Hughie was right" he thought, "The cops have nothing on me."

"That fucking Chandler, what was his first name? Sage? This is all his fault. Why the hell was he there? Who is he anyway? If he hadn't been there, everything would have gone off clean. Papa B and his whore would both be dead and Max wouldn't be lying in this hospital bed. "I'll get that fucker" Max thought.

Just then Hughie entered the room knocking as he opened the door. "Max?" he said, "How you doing?"

"Where the hell have you been, Hughie?"

"I stayed here the other night until after midnight, Max, but they wouldn't let me see you. They told me to go home."

Max glared at him sternly. "Yeah right" he said. "You're such a lying little fucker, Hughie."

Hughie looked at the floor to avoid a stare down with Max. He learned long ago that he'd never win a stare down against Max.

"Do you know that a cop came to visit me just now?" Max asked.

Taking a seat, Hughie faked his best stunned look, but Max saw right through his little charade of innocence.

"C'mon, Hughie" he said, "You know damn well why he was here."

"Mike's Place?" Hughie whispered.

"Yes. And you know what he wanted?"

Hughie thought about it for a moment. "Are we suspects, Max?"

Max frowned at Hughie. How could Hughie think *he* was a suspect? Nobody knew who Hughie was.

"Not *we*, Hughie" Max said. *Me.*

"Good" Hughie said. "It's best for both of us that no one knows about me."

"Well forget that for now, Hughie. I need you to look up some information for me."

Hughie sat forward in his chair so he could hear Max's very quiet voice. He didn't ask what Max wanted him to do. He knew Max would tell him soon enough. Max didn't like to be questioned. He'd divulge all the information he wanted anyone to know in his own time. Sometimes it took a while for Max to say what was on his mind.

"I want you to find all the information you can on a 'Sage Chandler'."

"Who is Sage Chandler?"

"He's the dirty bastard that shot me." Max held a finger to his lips to keep Hughie from asking questions.

"See what you can find out about him. Where he works and where he lives. Does he have any family? Anything."

Hughie was nodding in agreement. "OK" he said. "I'll start with the Internet and go from there."

Max waited for Hughie to say something more, but he didn't. Max said, "Why are you still here, then?"

With that Hughie stood and with a quick "good bye" to Max accompanied by a small wave of the hand, he was gone.

As Max watched the door close slowly behind Hughie, he hoped there would be a good deal of information on Chandler. "Sage Chandler" he whispered. It sounded vaguely familiar to Max, but it also sounded like an alias.

"Where have I heard that name before?" he wondered to himself.

He marveled at the stupidity of Papa storing the guy's real name in his cell phone. On the other hand, it would be kind of smart to come up with an alias for a contact. Or maybe that's the only name Papa knew this guy by. Maybe Chandler was shrewd enough to go by a nick name; something that couldn't be traced. Then again though, the name sounded so damn familiar. "Who the hell is Sage Chandler?"

The more he thought about it, the more Max began to suspect that "Sage Chandler" was an alias. He began to doubt that Hughie would find any information on that name, but one way or another, he would find this Chandler whoever he was and he would kill him.

Chapter 14

Hughie left the hospital immediately after leaving Max's room and was now driving back to the West Bottoms; back to the shit hole he and Max called home. There had been a push among the city leaders to start a renovation program in the West Bottoms area. It seems the area has a lot of history that could be an attraction for tourists. Other cities had done it, and now the Mayor and city council wanted to renovate the West Bottoms.

Thanks to the renovation project, someone had opened an Internet Cafe close enough where Hughie could get his laptop on-line from home. He'd had to install an extra powerful wireless card in his laptop, but now he was no able to achieve excellent connectivity from his home 300 yards away.

He entered the house, if you could call it that, and stood in the doorway. He looked in at the dilapidated walls, and rotting wood floors. The walls had been finished with lathe and plaster then covered in wallpaper. Now the wallpaper was hanging off the walls in places and the lathe and plaster was chipped and pealing. The roof had rotted in places and pieces of wood and masonry had fallen to the floor. Pigeon droppings lay on top of the debris.

Hughie wondered why he stayed here. Of course he knew why. If he were to leave, Max would find him unless he left the Midwest completely. Maybe he could hang out in Los Angles or Vegas for a while, but he didn't have the guts to travel that far by himself. He told himself it was his lack of money, but down deep he knew he'd never leave by himself. As shitty as the place was, and as crazy as Max was, he'd rather stay here than go someplace new.

He grabbed his laptop noting that the battery was fully charged. He fired up his Internet Browser and Goggled "Sage Chandler." He was amazed at the number of hits that matched his search criteria. There were several Sage Chandlers listed, many of whom he soon ruled out. One was an Artist, another a Senior Director for International Trade. That one he momentarily considered until he realized the guy lived in Washington DC. He continued his search. It wasn't until the second page of his Google search that he discovered a Sage Chandler from Kansas City.

But this couldn't be right. The Kansas City Chandler was a high profile attorney working at a prestigious law firm of Higgins, Rawlins, and Jones. The firm handled corporate law exclusively. What would this guy be doing in the West Bottoms at night?

Hughie continued his search finding similar information. Sage Chandler, it seemed, had been very successful at Higgins, Rawlins, and Jones. Many of the Internet stories were about Sage's successes, such as "Sage Chandler prevails for a prominent Missouri real estate broker in a breach of contract suit with a local contractor." There were numerous such entries touting Chandler's great successes.

"This is too easy" Hughie thought. "Can this really be the guy?"

He decided to search for Chandler's personal information. He was able to find Chandler's wife, Kim, and their two kids, Lisa and James. He discovered an address for Kim and even a phone number. He knew the area the address indicated. It was in a prestigious area of KC; the city's 'Snob Knob'." You have to have money to live there. No way someone with that kind of money would be caught dead in this shit hole part of town, especially at night. Something was not right about this. The more Hughie searched, the more he doubted this Sage Chandler was their guy. It didn't make any sense.

Suddenly he got an idea. He'd just call the phone number and see who answered. He dialed the number and waited. Someone answered on the third ring.

"Hello?" It was a female voice.

"Hello" Hughie said, "I would like to speak with Kimberly Chandler please?"

"Who is this?

"Oh my name is Larry Frank from the Nielson Television Rating Company. You have been selected as a Nielson family."

"Oh" Kim said, "I don't really watch much television. I'm not sure we'd be the best family to--"

Hughie cut her off. "It doesn't matter how much TV you watch, miss. if I can just verify some information we'll send you our packet."

She hesitated momentarily. Kim had become pretty cautious about giving out personal information. Being married to a high-profile attorney had taught her that you couldn't be too careful when it comes to divulging personal information.

"I assure you, ma'am" Hughie said. "We like to get a wide cross section of television viewers. It really doesn't matter if you don't watch television at all."

"OK" Kim said finally more out of exasperation and the desire to get off the phone than anything else. She considered just hanging up, but that would be rude, and she was trying to teach her children to avoid being rude.

"What information do you need?"

"Is your name Kimberly Chandler?"

"It used to be, but I'm divorced. 'Chandler' is my ex-husband's name."

"Oh, I'm sorry, Ma'am" Hughie said, "I didn't mean to interfere in your personal business. Do you reside at 810 Grand Elm Street?"

"Yes" she answered beginning to sound cheesed off.

"And how many televisions do you currently own?"

"Three"

"OK" Hughie said, "That's all I need. We will be sending you our information shortly. You should receive it in a few days. We will mail it to "Kim Chandler" unless you'd like to use another name at your current address."

"Chandler will fine" she said, "Is there anything else you need?"

"No. I will bid you a good day, Ma'am. Thank you very much for your time."

They said their goodbyes and Hughie hung up the phone.

So Chandler was no longer living with his wife. Hughie searched the Internet for an address for Sage Chandler, but he kept getting the same results: the same address Kim had verified on the phone. Well at least he had that, anyway. He would print some of the many pictures of the Chandlers he found listed on the Internet, and take them to Max. He wasn't exactly certain what Max had in mind, but he guessed he would appreciate this information although he would be pissed that Hughie hadn't found an exact address for Chandler himself.

Max had his own ways of finding people without using technology. Hughie never understood how he did it, but he had once seen Max go in search of a guy who'd borrowed money from him at forty five percent interest. The guy was late with his payment, and was trying to stay out of sight. It had only taken Max about 72 hours to track the guy down and beat him half to death for not having his money. He'd beaten him almost as bad as he'd beaten that poor bastard who'd been throwing his money around in Mike's Place that night over in Kansas.

Hughie left his shanty of a home, got in his car and returned to the hospital to show Max what he had found. He still had doubts about this being the Sage Chandler Max was looking for. It was hard to believe a high profile attorney would come to the shittiest part of town at 3:00 in the morning. Chances are, whoever this guy is, he knows that Chandler is a high-profile guy. He probably thought it would make a good alias on the street.

When he reached the hospital he went directly to Max's room and knocked on the door.

"Yeah" growled Max, "Come in."

Hughie entered the room and found Max alone. "Good" he thought.

"Well?" questioned Max, "Did you find anything?"

Hughie opened a manila envelope containing the pictures he'd printed of the Web pages he'd found.

"I did" he said, "but I'm not sure this is our guy." He extracted the pictures from the envelope and handed them to Max.

"What am I looking at?" Max questioned.

"Those are pictures of a high power attorney named Sage Chandler. He was the only Sage Chandler I could find from KC."

"Who's the dame?"

"That's his ex-wife. They are no longer married so she lives alone with their two kids." Max eyed the pictures carefully.

"So what makes you think this isn't our guy?"

"I just can't imagine why a guy like this would be hanging around the West Bottoms at night."

"Why not?"

Hughie defined some of Chandler's successes as a corporate attorney, where he lived, the circles he was affiliated with. "What would a guy like that be doing slinking around with a pimp at 3:30 in the morning?"

"Good point" Max said. "Still, it's the only lead we have right now. I'd like to follow up on it."

Hughie explained that he had the address of the Chandler home and he intended to setup surveillance outside the residence and wait until he could confirm the residents as being the same as the people in the pictures." He waited for Max to approve the idea before continuing.

"You have his address?" Max asked excitedly.

"No. I have the ex-wife's address."

"So you figure that you'll watch her place until you see these people in the pictures?"

"Yup. That pretty much sums it up."

Max wasn't sure he understood the logic of Hughie's plan. How was watching the guy's ex-wife's house going to help anything when he didn't know if they had the right guy to begin with?

"Even if you do match the people in the house with the people in the pictures, what have you got? We still don't know we got the right guy."

"Well... I have an idea about that?"

"You Hughie? You actually have a plan?" Max laughed at the thought of it. Hughie wasn't the plan man. He just carried out the technical part of Max's plans. That's the only reason Max kept him around. But today, Max was feeling generous. So he'd hear Hughie's plan. "This should be good for a laugh" he said. "OK, Hughie. Let's hear your plan."

Hughie detailed his plan to Max who listened intently. "It might be a little risky" Max said after hearing Hughie out, "but that's exactly what I was thinking of doing too."

Max instructed Hughie to go home and get some sleep. He told Hughie that even when the hospital released him, he wouldn't be going home right away.

"That cop" Max said. "That Marble. He said he'd be back when they release me from here."

Max explained that Marble would be back to take him downtown for a little Q & A session.

"But I think you're right, Hughie. I don't think they have anything on me so I should be out pretty fast."

Max almost wished they'd keep him in jail for a few days. His arm could use the rest before he and Hughie executed the plan.

He instructed Hughie to stay by his phone so when the cops did release him, Hughie could pick him up right away.

"If they do find something to pin on me, I'm gonna need you to post bond. So be where I can get in touch with you."

He further instructed Hughie not to come back to the hospital anymore, but to play it cool until he heard from Max.

"And Hughie" he said. "Don't get drunk, and don't go off with some hooker or dope dealer. I need you to stay straight."

"But don't you want me to check on the Chandler's house?"

"Yeah" Max said. "*Do* that, but don't do anything else, and don't get made or picked up for speeding or anything like that, and for Christ's sake, keep your cell phone with you."

Hughie assured Max that he would be available when needed. As if on cue the nurse entered the room.

"Time for a shave" she said.

"I was just leaving anyway" Hughie said and walked out of the room.

The nurse had brought in shaving cream, a disposable razor, a toothbrush and toothpaste. "Thought you might want to clean up a little" she said. She told Max to just lie back and she would handle the shaving part. She moistened his beard with a hot, damp washcloth and applied the shaving cream. As she shaved she asked how he was feeling.

"I actually feel pretty good today. When can I get outta here?"

"Probably tomorrow. The doctor will be around to see you in the morning and he'll let you know."

She finished shaving him, and wiped the excess shaving cream off with the damp washcloth. Then she filled the toothbrush and handed it to him. He brushed his teeth and rinsed with a glass of water the nurse handed him.

"Feel like getting up and around?" she asked.

Max had just been thinking about making his way to the bathroom. It was great timing really. She helped him swing his feet to the floor and to stand. Max walked toward the bathroom door. It didn't seem quite as far as it had the last time he'd made the journey.

The nurse helped him navigate the IV stand as he went through the bathroom door. He stood before the toilet and did his business. He was surprised at how much stronger he felt than he had the day before.

The nurse helped him back to the bed. "You're doing fine" she said. "I wouldn't be surprised if the doctor releases you tomorrow."

Max had mixed feelings about that. On one hand he wanted to get out of the hospital, but he also knew he wouldn't be going home right away. He wanted to be sure his strength was fully recovered before setting out after Chandler and it was much easier to rest in the hospital that it would be at a police station, especially if they put him in jail. But what would be, would be.

Chapter 15

The next day, Max awoke early. He felt good. He wanted to get out of this hospital bed, even if it meant going to jail. He was tired of the hospital bed. He was tired of dragging the IV stand around with him, and he was tired of hospital food.

The doctor came in early, right after breakfast. He checked Max's wound and the nurse who accompanied him, reapplied the bandage.

"Looks good" the doctor said. "You're healing nicely." He instructed the nurse to remove the IV and then asked Max to stand.

"Feel like a little walk?" he asked. "Before I can release you, you'll have to walk down the hall, up a flight of stairs and back."

That sounded kind of difficult to Max since the only walking he'd done since he arrived here was a few trips to the bathroom, but he wanted to leave.

"OK" Max said. "Let's do it."

The doctor and nurse helped Max to his feet. Walking was much easier without the cumbersome IV stand. He easily made his way to the doorway leading to the hallway, turned right and walked about 25 feet.

"OK. Stop." commanded the doctor. "Now turn right again and we'll see how you do with steps."

Max turned and with the nurse beside him, ascended the stairs. It was one of those split staircases with a landing half way up. Max climbed the ten steps leading to the landing one at a time. When he reached the landing, he was breathing pretty hard, and his heart was pounding which surprised him. The doctor, still standing at the bottom of the stairs, instructed him to rest there for a few breaths before he tried to return.

"You mean I don't have to go the rest of the way?"

"No. Just come on back down when you're ready."

He took a couple of deep breaths. With a firm grip on the handrail, he began his decent. One step at a time, ten steps later, he was back in the hallway on his way back to the hospital room.

The nurse lead him to his bed where he collapsed, breathing heavily, heart pounding again, and sweat beading on his scalp and forehead.

"Man" he breathed. "That was harder than I thought."

"But you did fine" the doctor said. "I think we can let you go this afternoon. If you have someone who will be coming to get you, you might want to call them."

Max had someone alright. He was surprised the doctor didn't know that. Then again maybe he was just saying what he always said to his patients prior to their release.

The doctor left the room and the nurse helped Max back to bed.

"Good news" she said excitedly. "You're going home."

"Yeah" Max replied half-heartedly. The nurse looked at him curiously. Most of her patients were pretty happy when they were released. What was the deal with this guy. Oh well, no business of hers.

"He'll probably let you go after lunch" she said. "Is there anything you need now?"

Max didn't need anything at that moment but some water. He'd worked up quite a thirst with his little walk. The nurse left for a few minutes and returned with a pitcher of ice water. She filled his huge, plastic mug with the hospital logo on the side.

"I will be back in a while" she said as she left the room.

After re-hydrating himself, and a short rest, Max felt pretty good. He got out of bed and looked out the hospital window. There wasn't much to see as his window viewed out onto the ceiling of another part of the hospital. He gathered his clothes together. He thought about getting dressed, but decided maybe he could talk the doctor into keeping him here another day or so. He'd been thinking about it and decided that staying in the hospital another day or two was probably a good idea. He didn't relish the idea of being thrown in jail with those street punks and losers. Normally, it wouldn't bother him, but he wasn't feeling normal. He might be vulnerable with his injured arm.

He heard the door open. He turned and watched a woman walk into the room. She was dressed more like a man than a man than a woman, in blue jeans, a polo shirt, and hiking boots. She displayed a badge on her belt, and was packing an automatic on her side.

"Hello Max" she said entering the room.

Max walked back to his bed, and climbed under the covers. "Hello" he returned.

"Looks like you got yourself into a little trouble here, Max."

"I got shot in the arm."

The woman walked to a chair beside the bed and took a seat. "You don't know who I am, do you Max?"

He remembered what Marble had said about Horniger retiring. "You're my Parole Officer."

"That's right Max" she said. "How did you know that? We've never met."

"That insignia on your shirt was a pretty good indication."

She looked down at the patch on her shirt. "Missouri State Department of Probation and Parole" it read.

"Good eyes. I wouldn't have thought you could read that from that distance."

Max didn't answer. He didn't admit that the patch was very familiar to him. He'd seen it before, several times, but this broad didn't need to know that.

"I'm Officer Susan Driscoll" she said. "I inherited you from my predecessor a few months ago."

"What happened to Hornigar?"

"He retired. I am his replacement."

Max lay there not asking any further questions. He knew better than to piss off the P.O. They have ultimate power over parolees. It's a stupid man who doesn't respect his P.O.

"We've been looking for you for a long time, Max" she said. "Why haven't you reported recently?"

"I am sorry about that, Susan, but I have been having some rough times."

"Please Max, refrain from using my first name. I am Officer Driscoll."   She paused and waited for acknowledgement but none came. She figured he was racking his brain for a good story. She didn't follow that line of questioning though.

"So what happened Max?" she asked instead. "Who shot you?"

"It was an accident" he said too quickly. "My roommate was cleaning his gun and it accidentally went off and he shot me."

Officer Driscoll asked about the roommate. She wanted to know his name, and how long Max had known him. She also wanted to know why the guy kept a gun in the house.

"Hughie is a veteran" Max explained. "He's really into guns and he's a little paranoid, so he likes to be armed." That was a lie. Hughie didn't want anything to do with guns. He was a medic in the Army. He was a pacifist at heart. When Hughie and Max first teamed up, Hughie wanted nothing to do with guns. Finally one day, Max broke into a residence and stole a .38 Special. He gave the revolver to Hughie and told him to have it with him always. Hughie 'forgot' it at home once when he and Max had stepped out and got a nasty belt to the face as a reward. Hughie never forgot his revolver again.

"So he's a gun collector?" she asked.

"No... Well, yeah, kind of... he has a small collection I guess."

Driscoll stood and walked around the room. Doesn't this guy know that when you live with a parolee you can't have weapons on the premises?"

"I guess we never discussed it."

Driscoll stared at Max. She knew he was lying, but she wasn't sure how far she wanted to push it. She wasn't sure a judge would revoke his parole for being shot in the arm. Besides, she wanted to get him on something bigger. Something that would put him away for a long time. She done some homework on Max. He was a bad one. She didn't really want to supervise him because she knew sooner or later he'd do something really bad. Something that would get someone hurt badly or even killed. She would have liked to get him locked up before that happened.

"Well now that you know" she began, "I expect he will be moving those weapons to another location."

Max agreed to ask Hughie to move his weapons to storage or to another location outside their home.

"Where do you live now, Max?"

"As I said, Officer, it's been rough. I'm basically living on the street."

"Well that's no way to live. Do you have a job?"

"Not at the moment." Max explained that he'd had a job until recently, but since the economy has tumbled, he'd been laid off. He's been unemployed for the last month or so.

"Well Max" she said, "Since I have no idea what kind of supervision you've had, I'm going to cut you a break." Driscoll said she would recommend that the judge not revoke his parole for being shot, or being in possession of weapons this time.

"But I am going to need to see you every day." she said. "You will be on close supervision for a while."

She also said she'd need to verify his address; that she and a police officer would take him to his residence after his questioning session with Marble.

"You will report every day, Max. If you miss one day, Max, I will be forced to put and ankle bracelet on you so I can keep track of you electronically."

Max said he understood. Driscoll thought he was full of shit, but had decided before arriving at the hospital that if she gave Max enough rope, he'd hang himself. They always did. Criminals are so predictable.

Driscoll had obtained a Masters in Psychology with an emphasis on the criminal mind from Northern Illinois University in DeKalb, Illinois. She'd been a cop, in Chicago and worked her way to detective. She knew the criminal mind through both education and experience. She quit the force to become a Parole Officer. It was safer than being a cop, and now that she was pushing 45 she figured it was time to get off the street, at least for the most part.

"Alright" she said finally. "I will see you at the questioning tomorrow that Detective Marble spoke to you about. I've been told that you will be released from here tomorrow morning right after breakfast."

She explained that she and Detective Marble would come to the hospital at nine o'clock sharp. "We will escort you to the Western Division Office where you will be detained for questioning."

With that she left. No goodbyes, no kiss my ass, nothing. "Well fuck you too" Max thought as the door slowly closed behind her. He didn't much like the idea of a female Parole Officer. Hornigar had been pretty easy, really. Max could miss appointments and call with some lame excuse and Hornigar always accepted them. Max could see this dame was going to be tougher to deal with. On the other hand, he could probably charm this woman, or if not, then surely he could intimidate her. Women were always intimidated by Max. Certainly this Susan Driscoll was no exception.

"So I'm outta here tomorrow" Max said to himself. That gave him another 12 hours or so of rest. He would sleep as much as possible during that time so he'd be mentally and emotionally ready for this questioning session.

"What did they think they were going to find?" Max had never squealed in his life. He was cool as a cucumber during questioning. They couldn't have sent him to prison on the circumstantial evidence alone. If that little chicken shit Smith hadn't sold him out in a damn plea agreement, they wouldn't have had a case at all.

It was all Smith's idea to rob that convenience store and rape the cashier. That damn Smith. Max would not have hurt that girl, but Smith just had to beat her up. "She won't talk if we kick the shit out of her" he'd said. "She'll be too scared." Then he knocked her down and kicked her in the head. He said he hadn't meant to kill her, just scare her good, but that kick to the head fractured her skull and drove the bone into her brain.

They didn't even get out of the store before the cops came. It had taken them too long to rob, rape, and kill the girl. They were apprehended red-handed. Then Smith crayfished on the witness stand saying Max had been the one to deliver the fatal blow. Max was sent to prison on Manslaughter, and Smith got off with a suspended sentence. Never did any time at all, and he was the one who'd killed the girl.

Smith was the one guy who'd gotten away. While Max was doing his time, Smith found somewhere else to live. Max searched, notified other people with whom he was affiliated at the time who were very good at locating people, but no one ever found Smith. Max had always wondered if he'd gone into witness protection or something. Max consoled himself with the thought that someone had killed the bastard. Wherever he was, he was gone and it burned Max to think he might still be alive, so he chose not to think about Smith very often.

Just then Max got a bad feeling. "What if Hughie is another Smith?" he though. Max didn't see any reason why they'd haul Hughie in for questioning. Neither Marble or Driscoll had asked about Hughie. On the other hand, that might be a ploy too, meant to knock Max off guard when he enters the police station and finds Hughie already there. "Shit!" Max thought. Hughie is weak when it comes to this kind of thing. He probably wouldn't be able to endure the good cop/bad cop routine. He doubted that Hughie had ever sat through one of those sessions. When Hughie was sent up, it was on a nonviolent computer crime of some kind. Hughie had copped a plea bargain because the evidence was so strong against him. The authorities had confiscated his computer before he could erase the incriminating files. He was fucked and he knew it so he took the plea.

But this was different. If they called Hughie in for questioning, Max felt Hughie would get tripped up by the cops' tactics and panic. He could only hope for now that the cops were not suspicious of Hughie.

Chapter 16

The next morning Max was up early. The nurse brought breakfast at 7:30 am. He ate hungrily. "I must be getting better" he thought. His appetite had returned with a vengeance.

After finishing his breakfast, he propped himself up on two pillows and turned on the television. The only thing he found that he could stand to watch was the game show network. Match Game was on. He'd always liked the Match Game. The sexual innuendos were still funny, but he assumed young people these days wouldn't think so since anything goes on TV now.

He watched TV and waited for the doctor to arrive. He finally came in about 8:15. He examined Max's wound and redressed it.

"I believe you can go home anytime you want" he said.

Max figured the doctor must know that he was being picked up by the authorities. "So I can just walk out of here anytime I want?"

"Well no. The police are coming to give you a ride. Didn't they tell you?"

"Yeah. They told me."

The doctor said Max could get dressed anytime he pleased and left without further comment. Max continued watching TV until 8:45 and then decided he probably better get ready to go.

Driscoll and Marble showed up at 9:00 on the dot.

"You ready, Max?" Driscoll asked.

He said he was, and hefted his plastic bag full of things he'd acquired during his stay. There was the huge plastic mug he'd been drinking water from, and a toothbrush. There was the breathing thing they'd made him use every hour so he wouldn't get pneumonia.

"Its hell of a deal that they can force you to buy this crap isn't it?" he said. Neither Driscoll nor Marble said anything.

"Yup. It's a hell of a thing" Max said again. A new nurse arrived with a wheelchair and asked that Max be seated.

"I can walk" Max said. The nurse shook her head. "Hospital rules" she said.

Max lowered himself into the wheelchair and the trio left the hospital room with the nurse pushing Max in the wheelchair. They walked down the hall to the elevator. They all piled in and Driscoll hit the button marked '1'. When the elevator stopped they exited, Max in the wheelchair, the nurse who provided propulsion, Driscoll, and Marble. They stopped at the front desk.

"You're all checked out Mr. Brown" said an older nurse behind the desk.

Max thought it was interesting how easily one could check out of a hospital if he had the right connections. Still, they wouldn't let him leave on foot without the wheelchair. They exited the front doors and the nurse wheeled Max to a black Ford Crown Victoria parked in the ambulance zone.

"Unmarked car" Max thought as he was ushered into the rear set. Marble got in the driver's side as Driscoll opened the passenger door and climbed in. Max sat in the back. They had not cuffed him, but there was a strong mesh screen surrounded by bullet-proofed glass between the front and rear seats. He was glad they had not cuffed him.

Driscoll turned around to face Max. "Take us to your home, Max" she said. "I want to see where you are living." Max was reluctant to begin with.

"The place is such a mess" he said. "I'd be ashamed to show you where I live."

"I need to see it, Max."

Max eyed Driscoll. He could see she was not one to mess with. She was different from most women, he could see that. She was tough. She'd send his ass back to prison in a heartbeat if he disobeyed, and although prison didn't frighten him, Max was in no hurry to return to the joint. Still he didn't want to show her where he and Hughie lived. There were weapons there and probably booze knowing Hughie.

"I ain't afraid of prison" he said.

"Good" Driscoll said without hesitation. "Cause I ain't afraid to send you there."

He sat back and studied on his situation for a while. If he took her home and they searched the place, they'd find the guns and who knows what else. She might send him away. On the other hand, if he refused, she'd definitely try to revoke his parole due to noncooperation.

"Fine" he said finally. "Take a right on the light."

Marble drove to the next stop light and stopped. "Hang a right here?"

"Yup" Max said. "Then just take this street all the way to the end.".

"That will lead us to the West Bottoms"

"That's right."

"What are the West Bottoms?" Driscoll asked.

"It's the oldest part of town" Marble explained. "Just a bunch of old warehouses, and stock yards mostly."

"Why are you living there, Max?"

"Because Officer Driscoll, times have been hard lately. Been outta work for a few months now."

They drove for a long time without speaking further and arrived in the West Bottoms after about 30 minutes. Max directed Marble to the hovel. Hughie's car was in the front. Max was hoping that Hughie saw them pull up and was busy hiding evidence.

"Let's take a look at this joint" said Driscoll opening the car's back door for Max.

"OK" Max said getting out of the car. "But it ain't pretty."

Max led the way to the front door and entered. Hughie hadn't seen or heard them. He was sitting in a rotting recliner drinking a beer.

"Oh" he said. "Hi Max. I didn't know you were coming home today."

"Good line, Hughie" Max thought. It might squelch any ideas that Max had contacted Hughie before leaving the hospital. On the other hand, maybe it came off as rehearsed.

Max introduced Driscoll and Marble to Hughie. "Hughie Long" Marble said. "That name rings a bell."

Hughie explained that he had done a little time in KSP for credit card theft by way of computer back in the 90s.

"So are you on parole too?" Driscoll asked.

"No. Not anymore. My probation ended six months ago. I am a free man."

Driscoll instructed Hughie to stand up so Marble could frisk him. "We need to make sure you're not packin'" she said.

"Packin' what?" Hughie asked as he worked his way out of the beat up old chair.

When he finished his search, Marble told Hughie to sit back down and then instructed Max to have a seat as well. The only other furniture was an broken down old couch that looked more like a love seat as Max sat down. With Max and

Hughie both seated, Driscoll and Marble began tossing the place.

"What a shithole this place is" said Marble.

Driscoll agreed. "I don't see how people can live like this." They looked in the room that Driscoll figured must function as a bedroom. There was an old, stained mattress on the floor, a laptop computer in its case, and an ashtray full of cigarette butts on top of an old wooden crate. Marble opened the computer case and found nothing but a laptop computer and the power supply.

Driscoll entered a room that appeared to be the kitchen. There was a pretty large cooler on the floor she figured the men used as their refrigerator. She opened the cooler and found it partially stocked with beer cans, a couple cans of cola, and an unopened quart of milk.

Returning to the room where Max and Hughie were seated, Driscoll said "you can't have this beer here, Hughie. Not with Max living here."

"But" Hughie began, "I told you I am no longer on probation. Why can't I have beer?"

"You can. But not with Max living here."

She was about to return to her search when Marble appeared from the bedroom. "Nothing" he said. "Clean as a whistle other than a laptop computer."

Driscoll informed Marble of the beer in the cooler. There weren't any other rooms to search. Just the living room, the one bedroom and the kitchen.

"Alright" Driscoll said. "I guess there is nothing else here." Turning toward Max she said "I have no jurisdiction over Hughie. If he wants to live here that's his business, but you Max, you cannot live in a place like this."

"But I told you" he said, "I have no money no place else to go."

"Well you're going to find employment and move into a decent place once your arm is fully recovered."

"I've been looking... I can't find a job. Neither can Hughie."

"Well we're gonna arrange for a nice, comfortable room for you for the next few days."

"Jail? Why?"

"For violation of your parole for starters. We'll see what turns up in the meantime."

They escorted Max out the door and back to the unmarked car and drove to the Kansas City Police Station: Western Division. It wasn't Max's first visit. He'd been hauled in on several occasions for various charges. He felt pretty secure. He knew they had nothing on him and couldn't hold him for very long. He'd just make the best of it for now and he'd be out within 72 hours probably. Meanwhile, his arm would have a chance to heal. Jail wasn't the ideal place to convalesce but it would do.

Marble parked the car and he and Driscoll exited the vehicle. Driscoll opened the rear passenger door and asked Max to remove himself. Max made a show of getting out of the car. His arm did hurt, but not nearly as much as he made out. Once out of the car, Driscoll grabbed him by his good arm.

"We are going inside now Max" she said. "If you struggle we're gonna cuff you... Is that understood?"

Max agreed that he did understand and let Officer Driscoll escort him. He went along easily. He didn't want to be cuffed behind his back. He knew that would be painful given the condition of his shoulder. The officers lead him inside the station, past the front desk and directly to a jail cell. They pushed him inside the cell and locked the door.

"Wait a minute" Max protested.

"Aren't we gonna book him first?" Driscoll asked.

"We've booked him a number of times. We've got his finger prints on file and a fairly recent photo. We know all about him."

The normal procedure was to shower and delouse the prisoner, strip search and dress him in the orange coveralls supplied by the county, and then he's off to booking. But since Max had just been released from the hospital, Marble figured they could dispense with the shower and delousing.

Marble turned to Max who looked at him through the bars of the jail cell. "You're being held for violation of your parole" Marble said. "You are also a person of interest in an on-going criminal investigation. Just sit tight and someone will be along with your jail clothes. Driscoll and I will be back to get you within the hour."

Max thought maybe this was some kind of violation of his civil rights. "I want to see my lawyer" he said.

"You don't need a lawyer" Driscoll said. "You're a Parolee with a gunshot wound, Max. That alone is enough for us to hold you, so just cool your jets."

Max let go of the bars on the cell door he'd been holding. He knew Driscoll was right. She could send him back to prison easily enough. He had evaded his Parole Officer for three months. That alone was enough to revoke his parole. Plus the gunshot wound which was at best a direct violation. Just being in possession of a gun was grounds to revoke him. He decided to just shut up and get through this.

Max turned and looked at the bunk beds in his cell. He shared the cell with no one, yet, which he thought was fortuitous. He didn't need some punk giving him a hard time with this bad arm. He stepped to the lower bunk and lay down. "Just relax" he thought to himself. "They've got nothing on you."

Just then another officer, probably the jailer, Max thought, came and held an orange jump suit through the bars. Put this on and hand your street clothes and all personal items to me through the bars." Max did as he was instructed and lay back on the bunk.

Max had been in the cell no more than an hour before Marble came to escort him to an interrogation room. Max rolled out from his lower bunk on Marble's command.

"Let's talk, Max" Marble said. He opened the cell door. Max moved forward and through the cell door. It wasn't until he was on the other side that Max realized that Marble wasn't alone. Two armed guards, one on each side of the cell, stood with their automatic pistols trained on Max.

"We're just taking every precaution, Max" Marble said. "Just do as I say and everything will be fine."

Max exited the cell and with one guard in front of him and one guard behind, he was escorted down a long hallway into an small room with a table with several chairs surrounding it.

"Sit" Marble said indicating a chair at the table.

"I feel a little like Hannibal Lecter" Max said sitting down.

"Good" Marble answered. "We're treating you a little like Hannibal Lecter."

Max was suddenly surprised they hadn't strapped a muzzle on him and wheeled him in on a hand truck. He felt a little insulted that these cops would see him as such a monster.

"Come on guys" he said. "I'm not a cannibal."

Without responding, Driscoll and Marble sat down in chairs strategically positioned on the other side of the table from where Max was sat. The armed officers stood on each side of Max, weapons drawn.

"Alright" Marble said. "We need to ask you some questions pertaining to an incident at a little bar called Mike's Place on the night of October seventh."

Max looked back and forth between Driscoll and Marble. "We have two witnesses who have placed you at the scene that night."

"Yeah" Max began. "I was there."

"Were you drinking?" Driscoll asked.

Max admitted that he and Hughie had a few beers, but weren't drunk by any means. "There was a man there buying round after round for the house."

"Did you know this man?" Marble asked.

"No. I had never seen him before and probably wouldn't recognize him today."

Producing an envelope from his jacket pocket, Marble said "Lets see about that." He pulled several pictures from the envelop and laid them on the table before Max. "Do you recognize him now?"

In all the pictures the man had been beaten so badly he was hardly recognizable as a human. Marble thought that seeing the badly beaten man might cause Max some discomfort, but Max showed no emotion whatsoever.

"I don't think that's the guy" Max said.

"What guy?"

"The guy who was buying all the drinks."

Marble and Driscoll exchanged a quick glance. "We didn't tell you that the man in these photos is the man who was buying all the drinks, Max."

"Well..." hesitated Max, "I just assumed... since he had money." Max turned his attention to the pictures making a big show of pondering each one diligently. "This sure don't look like him to me" he said. "Course it's hard to tell all beat up the way he is."

Max stopped looking at the photos and sat back in his chair with his hands folded on the table. He sat quietly waiting for the next question.

"Come on, Max!" Marble shouted. "You did this to this man and you know it."

"No. Hughie and I left early. Ask your witnesses."

"We did. They said you left around eleven-thirty or so."

"And when was this man attacked?"

"Around closing time; 1:30 am or thereabouts."

So how could I have done this?"

Marble didn't answer. He just sat and glared at Max who was sitting comfortably in his chair with a slight smile on his face.

"OK. Fine, Max. How about explaining what you know about a shooting in the West Bottoms a few nights back."

"Me? Nothing. I hadn't even heard about it until you guys told me the other day. In case you've forgotten, I've been in the hospital."

"Yes you have. And how did you get shot, Max? What were you doing?"

"You know that area, Detective. Its filled with undesirables of all kinds. There were three punks who tried to rob me on my way home."

"What?" Marble asked. "You said in the hospital that you shot yourself accidentally."

"Yeah, but that's not what really happened."

"So you were lying then?" asked Driscoll.

"I lied to you Detective because..." Max paused racking his brain for something that sounded plausible. Driscoll and Marble exchanged a quick glance. They didn't need to speak. Both understood the body language. Driscoll decided to add some pressure.

"Why did you lie, Max? Come on!"

"I don't know if either of you have ever been shot, but I can tell you its no fun. When you're laying there in pain and half doped up on morphine you don't feel much like telling a long story."

"But why tell a lie that can get your parole revoked?" asked Driscoll.

"Well that must have been the morphine. I wasn't thinking clearly."

Marble stood and walked behind Max. He didn't say anything for a long time. Driscoll wasn't sure what kind of tactic Marble was using, but she didn't speak either. Finally Marble said, "OK so you were walking home you say... home from where?"

Max didn't answer immediately. Marble repeated his question.

"I'd just gone out for a walk and these three punks..."

"Why would you go for a walk at night in a part of town that you yourself describe as being full of undesirables?"

"I was just restless. Hughie and I have nothing to do, no TV, no radio. It gets kind of boring, you know?"

"Did Hughie go walking with you?"

"No."

"You are lying, Max!"

"No. I am not."

"Tell us what happened to your arm!"

Max repeated his story. Three punks jumped him and tried to rob him, but he had nothing on him. He was broke. That seemed to anger the punks and so they shot him in the arm for not having any money they could steal.

"You expect us to believe that?"

"It's the truth."

"Its bullshit, Max, and you know it." No one talked for a few moments. Marble had either run out of questions or was tired of getting the same bullshit answers.

"I can send you back to prison, Max" Driscoll interjected suddenly. "You know that, right?"

Max indicated that he was fully aware of the power Driscoll had over him. "I'm being honest with you, Officer Driscoll. I admitted to being at that bar, and to drinking a few beers. I don't know anything about this poor man in the pictures here or about any murder in the West Bottoms. I was shot by three punks who were trying to rob me."

"Well I think you know more than you're telling us, Max" she said, "but be that as it may, I am not going to send you to prison."

Max looked relieved. It was the first sign of any emotion that he'd shown since being brought into the interrogation room.

"Thank you" he said softly.

"At least, not yet. You and I have no history, Max, and since Hornigar didn't fill me in on you, all I have to go on is your file. So you and I are going to get to know one another and like I said, you will get a job and find a decent place to live."

"Yes Ma'am."

"And you will report to me daily for the first month of our relationship. I want to keep an eye on you."

"Yes Ma'am."

"If you miss one day, we will find you and you will go to jail."

"Yes Ma'am."

"I am going to hold you here for 72 hours for your parole violation. These nice officers will escort you back to your cell now."

Turning to the officers she said, "Cuff him."

The two armed officers cranked Max's arms behind his back. Max groaned in pain, but Driscoll didn't bite. She thought he was probably being overly dramatic, but if it did hurt? Good.

"The cuffs are too small" said one of the officers. "We need an over-sized set. Anyone got any?"

Marble looked around the interrogation room but there were no large cuffs.

"To hell with the cuffs" Driscoll said. "Just take him to his cell and if he makes a wrong move, just shoot him."

After the officers had taken Max out of the room, Driscoll watched the door slowly close. "He's a cold one, isn't he?"

"Oh yeah" Marble said. "You don't turn your back on Maxwell Brown. But why didn't you revoke his parole? Lord knows you have plenty of reasons."

Driscoll stood and paced the room. "I thought seriously about it" she said, "but if I send him away on a parole violation, he'll be out in a year, maybe less. I want to put that bastard away for a good, long time."

"Yeah" Marble said as he backed away from the table and stood. "He is definitely a menace to society. I'd like to see him locked away for a long time."

Driscoll stopped pacing and sat down opposite of Marble in the chair where Max had sat. "I could order a psychological evaluation" she said, "but the outcome would be antisocial personality, and we already know that."

"Yeah" Marble agreed. "He's the most antisocial personality I've ever dealt with. So what do we do?"

"We give him enough rope and let him hang himself."

"How do you mean?"

"I can hold him for 72 hours for his admission to drinking. In the meantime, maybe some new evidence will turn up concerning Max. If not, we release him. He'll screw up eventually if I give him a long enough leash. Then we'll have him on something solid and can send him away for a good long time."

Chapter 17

Three days later Driscoll and Marble had turned up no new evidence linking Max to any crimes. Driscoll was seriously considering changing her mind and filing for a revocation hearing. At least then he'd be off the streets for a while. Maybe if luck was on their side, Max would commit some sort of crime in prison and receive some extra time, but she doubted it. She'd done some research over the past few days and found that Max was a model prisoner, or appeared so officially. He was smart enough to know how to do his time and get out as quickly as possible. She'd even met with Marble to discuss the options.

"I agree with your original idea" Marble said. "If you revoke him, he'll be out in a year or so. It would just be a bandage."

"Yeah, that's how I still see it too." said Driscoll.

That afternoon the armed officers went to get Max from his cell and escort him back to the same interrogation room where he had met with Driscoll and Marble before.

"Sit down, Max" Driscoll commanded.

The three resumed their positions at the table with an armed officer on each side of Max.

"Who shot you Max?" Marble asked wasting no time.

"I told you, Detective. Three punks tried to rob me."

"Yeah right. The hole in that story is bigger than the hole in your arm." Max said nothing. He just sat there looking straight ahead with his hands folded on the table.

"Who shot you?" Driscoll demanded. "Tell us the truth!"

Max didn't even flinch. He just sat there hands folded on the table.

"Well" began Driscoll, "I have been considering a revocation hearing. "

"What?" Max shouted. No she had his attention. "You already promised you wouldn't send me back."

"I didn't promise you shit!" She leaded very close to Max and placed her hand on her holster and popped the flap open. "Max" she said just above a whisper. "Do you have a ride home?"

It wasn't what Max expected her to say. It knocked him off guard briefly. "What?"

"Do you have a ride home, Max?" she repeated this time with much more force than before.

"Yes... Hughie could... are you done grilling me about my arm?"

Driscoll stood up straight and backed off. "You won't tell us anything. We could grill you all day and you'd just keep lying." Driscoll looked at the guards. Take him to a phone so he can call one of his lowlife friends to come get him."

"But..." Max mumbled. "I thought you guys would take me home. You brought me here."

"We've been to your home, Max" Marble said. "I ain't in any hurry to go back."

Marble looked at one of the armed officers. "Take him to a phone, then throw him back in a cell until someone comes for him."

The officers pulled Max to his feet. In the process the officer on the right pulled on Max's injured arm, and Max howled in pain. In truth, however, Max was surprised that it barely hurt at all. His arm was healing. It would be good as new in a few more days.

The officers let Max make his call, then took him back to his cell. After a few minutes, an officer brought his street clothes. He was dressed and lay on the lower bunk. Hughie arrived about thirty minutes later.

As they left the Police Station, Hughie ran to his car and pulled it to the front doors so Max wouldn't have to walk so far. Max clumsily got inside Hughie's little car. It was a tight fit, but Max finally got himself folded into the passenger side.

"So where's the money?" Max asked.

"While you were still in the hospital, I got a feeling I better stash it. Don't worry Max. The money is safe. I took it to the Crane building and stashed it in a hole in the ceiling of the second floor. Our guns are right there in the jockey box."

"Good play, Hughie... So what have you found out about Chandler?" Max asked after Hughie had begun driving.

"Oh, I've got good news for you there, Boss."

Chapter 18

A few days later, Samantha and I were on our way to the police station to see if she could identify her kidnapper. Traffic was heavy for some reason making travel slow. We didn't talk much after we dialed in an old classic country station on the radio of my 1998 Oldsmobile. It was a boat, but I liked it. It made me feel safer because it was so much bigger and heavier than anything else around me.

"I like this station" Samantha said as I turned right off Main onto Linwood Avenue. "They play a lot of good old country music."

"Yeah" I replied, "I listen to it all the time."

It wasn't long before we arrived at our destination. I parked the car and we crossed the street to the Kansas City, Missouri Police Department, Central Division.

We entered the station and made our way to the front desk. The place was very active I thought. I'd been here many times years ago and I didn't remember this much activity.

"Crime must be flourishing" I said.

There were cops sitting at desks talking on their phones, hookers sitting around waiting for something or someone cops bringing suspects in, or moving them somewhere. There were cops taking statements from regular citizens who had been victimized by muggers or violated in some other way.

Two cops came right by us with a male suspect between them. The suspect was handcuffed behind his back and the two men were leading him somewhere. The man was struggling and shouting as he passed.

"Fucking pigs. I didn't do anything. You've got the wrong man."

"Watch your language, sir" one of the cops said. "There are decent people here who don't want to listen to that kind of language."

We approached the front desk. The woman behind the bullet-proof glass wore a regular cop's uniform with a badge pinned to her chest and two stripes on each arm. There was a four inch hole in the glass with a mesh over to allow communication. The name plate on the desk read "Corporal Eileen Mullen." She was a short, husky woman, with short, dark hair and eyes that were almost black. She looked as though she might be of Hispanic heritage, at least partially.

"Can I help you?" she asked.

"We are here to see Sergeant Bill Jenkins."

"You mean Lieutenant Jenkins?"

"Ah... yes. He's a Lieutenant now"?

Yes he is" she said after typing a few keys on her computer. "Who should I say is calling?"

Not really wanting to give my name because it tends to cause people to ask the same old "are-you-the-same-Sage-Chandler-who" question, I said, "Uh, just tell him we might have information about the murder in the West Bottoms."

She picked up the phone and dialed three numbers. "Detective" she began, "There are two people here to see you. They say they have information on the West Bottoms murder." She paused a moment. "Okay" she said into the phone and hung up.

"He'll be right out, sir" she said and went about her business shuffling through papers and typing on her computer. We just stood there waiting.

"You can have a seat while you wait" she said pointing to a row of armless chairs in a nook designated as a waiting room.

"No thanks" I replied. "We'll just stand here and wait." I knew she wanted us to move away from the window, but I didn't want to. I didn't want to mingle with the criminals and losers who were sitting around here and there. Nor did I feel like sitting around with a bunch of victims either.

Vics tend to bring me down. They remind me that we live in a world with really shitty people who are just waiting to take advantage of any pour soul they can. They are vultures who prey on the weak. So we just stood there watching Mullen go about her business. I knew we were making her uncomfortable, but I didn't care. She didn't suffer long because not two minutes later, Lieutenant Bill Jenkins popped through the door.

"Sage?" he said tentatively walking over and shaking my hand. "Long time, no see, buddy. Where you been"

"Hey Bill" I replied. "Oh, I've been around."

"Man Sage" he said. "What's it been? Three years?"

"Yeah, at least three" I answered. "So you made Lieutenant, huh?"

"Yeah, a year ago now. Its Detective Jenkins now" he said beaming and pointing to his shield.

"Well good. Good for you, Bill." He smiled and glanced at Samantha.

"Oh yeah" I said, "I'm sorry. This is Samantha Johnson, a friend of mine."

"Hello Ms. Johnson" Bill said, gently shaking her hand. He took one step back and looked me up and down, glanced over at Samantha for a moment then back to me. "You look pretty good, Sage" he said. "It's really good to see you. You must be doing pretty good for yourself these days.

"Oh I'm getting by, Bill."

He stood there smiling for a moment more. "Come on back to my office and we'll get some coffee."

He turned and lead the way to the door through which he had only minutes before appeared.

"Know him?" I asked Samantha while we followed."

"No" she said, "I've never met this one."

We followed him to his office. He sat at his desk and motioned for us to sit in the chairs on the other side of his desk.

He picked up his phone and dialed someone. "Can we get some coffee in here please?" he asked. "Thank you."

"We'll have some coffee in here soon.... So how have you been? You look great."

"I've not been too bad, Bill" I answered. "I've become a private investigator since I last saw you."

Bill looked surprised, and I could tell he was doing his best to suppress a laugh. "You Sage?" he said finally, "A private investigator?"

"Yeah" I said, "go on Bill. You can laugh if you want." But Bill had gotten control of himself by then. "No" he said, "I think that's great. Had any adventures yet?"

"Actually yes" I said, "That's why we've come to see you."

Just then the short, dark haired Corporal Mullen arrived with the coffee. She set a tray containing a carafe, three cups, packets of sugar and dried cream with spoons on a table beside the chair I was sitting in. She poured a cup and asked Samantha if she wanted cream or sugar. "No thank you" Samantha answered, "black is just fine."

"Me too" I chimed in before Mullen could ask. She poured cups for each of us and handed them to us one by one.

"Thank you, Mullen" Bill said. She nodded, turned and left the office. Since I was closest to the tray, Bill asked me for one cream and one sugar. I handed them to him along with a spoon and we all took a sip of our coffee.

"So where were we?" Bill asked.

"I was telling you about the adventures of Sage Chandler" I said. Bill nodded his approval. "Oh yeah. So tell me."

I relayed the whole story leaving out only the fact that I had shot the kidnapper. It was a bit tough telling Bill that Samantha was actually Trixy Bedluv, a prostitute who worked for Papa B, but the news didn't seem to faze him.

"So" Bill said turning his attention to Samantha, "can you identify this guy who shot Papa B?"

"Maybe" she began, "I am not sure. I never got a really good look at him. He's frigging huge, I can tell you that."

"Very big man, huh?"

"Frigging huge" she repeated.

"Well, I'll get Mullen to bring in the mug book and we'll see if you recognize any one. You never know, someone might jump out at you." He called Mullen again and asked that she bring the Mug book in. Most cops used their computers to look at mug shots that were saved on State and Federal databases, but Bill was an old school kind of guy. He preferred the old fashioned mug book, especially when the suspect was likely a local.

Mullen brought the book in and handed it to Bill. "Here you are, Lieutenant" she said. "Is there anything else I can do for you sir?"

"No" Bill answered. "That'll be all. Thank you."

"Are you sure? Cause it's kind of busy out there." If he noticed her sarcastic attitude, he didn't let on. Without looking up or repeating himself, he opened the book, turned in upside down and slid it over to Samantha. "Take your time, Miss" he said. I was watching Samantha as she examined each picture intently before moving to the next. I waited until Mullen left the office.

"Bill?" I said, "While Samantha is looking at the book here, can I speak with you in private?" Samantha glared at me. I knew she wondered why I felt I had to speak in private. "I'll tell you later" I said. "Just look at the book and I'll be right back."

"Certainly" Bill answered. We left Bill's office and finally found a private interrogation room that was unoccupied. No one else was around, so we entered the room. As soon as he'd closed the door Bill said, "We might get run outta here because we're so busy today, so we'd better make this quick. What is it?"

I studied Bill for a moment. Could I still trust him now that he'd made Lieutenant? I decided to just jump right in.

"I shot him, Bill" I blurted.

"Shot who?" he asked.

"The kidnapper. I shot him. I'm not sure where I hit him, but I know I hit him."

"Wait a minute" he said. "You shot him?" I nodded "Yeah I hit him too but, I'm not sure where exactly... In the arm maybe."

"Do you know a Detective by the name of Jack Marble?" he asked.

"Marble" I mouthed a few times. "No can't say that I do."

"He's been around a few years. He's with the Western Division."

I had worked almost exclusively with the Central Division when I worked with Law Enforcement. They handled the white collar crime along with the lighter criminal cases. The Western Division tended to handle more of the really nasty stuff like murder and rape.

"So what about him?" I asked.

"Well he questioned a guy in the hospital with a bullet wound in his upper arm."

"Oh really" I asked. "A really big son of a bitch?"

"Yeah, Max is huge, stands six foot six or so and weighs probably two-fifty, maybe two-sixty.

"I suppose he could be our man, but aren't gunshot wounds fairly common around here?"

"Yes. But not at the Shawnee Mission Medical Center." Bill explained that it was strange that Max had ended up at Shawnee rather than County. Shawnee is much more expensive. "I doubt Max has insurance." he said. "I'm surprised they admitted him at Shawnee."

"He might not have insurance" I said, "but he does have fifty thousand dollars in cash, six of which was supposed to be my fee."

Bill looked at me strangely. "So that's what you want? Your six grand?" I assured Bill that I was not interested in the money.

"I'd like to see this guy put away for shooting Papa, and especially for what he did to Samantha."

Bill nodded. "He is one no good son of a bitch" he said. "It's a shame you didn't shoot him in the head. He's probably the meanest bastard I've ever dealt with."

"I was aiming for his head," I said, "but I missed because I was shooting with my left hand. Who is he anyway?"

"His name is Maxwell Brown, but he's got a bunch of aliases. You don't want to mess with this guy, Sage."

"Has he got a rap sheet?"

"Oh yeah. A long one. Rape, aggravated assault, and robbery mostly." Bill explained that Max had done almost eight years at Kansas State Prison a few years ago for assault and robbery, and manslaughter. "We also suspect that he is guilty of a murder over in Kansas, but can't prove it."

"Well if he's the same guy, he murdered Papa B. I saw him do it." Bill strode to an interview table and sat down. He gestured for me to join him.

"He's got a sidekick too" Bill said. "He's a computer hacker by the name of Hughie Long. Ever heard of him?"

The name sounded vaguely familiar. Bill shrugged and continued his explanation.

Hughie and Max met in prison. Hughie was doing time for hacking into a credit card company computer and ripping them off for two hundred and fifty thousand.

"Oh" I interjected. "I do remember that. *This* guy is *that* guy?"

"Yeah" Bill said. "He managed to transfer two hundred and fifty thousand into a bank account he'd set up just for that purpose. The money was never recovered."

He looked at the floor and kicked at an imaginary rock or something.

"You're not gonna want to hear this, Sage" he said, "but we had him. We had him in jail on a parole violation."

"Had him?" I asked. "Had who? This Hughie guy?"

"No. Maxwell Brown... Well we didn't have him here, but Marble picked him up when the hospital released him yesterday. The bad news is we had to let him go this morning."

I didn't answer. I just stood there listening to Bill fill in the details. "He'd been wanted for routine questioning" Bill said, "for an assault and robbery over in Kansas." Bill relayed the whole story about the assault and robbery and that two witnesses were able to place Brown and Miller at the scene, but they both said they'd watched them leave at least an hour before the robbery."

"Damn it!" I exclaimed. "Are you sure this is the same guy?"

"Well we'll see if your girl picks anyone out, but I'll lay odds that if she does, it'll be Maxwell Brown."

I was very disappointed. If Samantha and I had arrived a day earlier or even hours earlier she could have fingered the bastard. Bill must have sensed my disappointment.

"We had no choice but to release him, Sage, We just didn't have any evidence... nothing to hold him on."

"He's got my cell phone number, Bill" I said at last. Bill looked stunned.

"What?" he said. "How the hell did he get that?" I told him that Papa must have saved my number in his cell phone under my real name because the guy had called me "Mr. Chandler."

"He obviously has Papa's cell phone" I said.

"What did his voice sound like?" asked Bill.

I thought momentarily trying to remember. "It was a low, gravelly voice; he spoke almost in whispers sometimes."

"That's not good news, Sage" he said, "If I were you, I'd think seriously about getting a new phone number." I nodded and shrugged my shoulders in acknowledgement.

"Seriously, Sage."

We left the interrogation room and returned to Bill's office where Samantha sat staring at a picture intently. We entered an took our seats.

"Do you recognize anyone?" Bill asked.

Samantha nodded her head slowly and looked up at me. "I think so" she said. "This guy." She turned the book around and sure enough, the name beneath the picture said "Maxwell Brown." Bill gave me a knowing glance.

"Are you sure, Miss?" Bill asked looking at Samantha.

"Yes I am" she said. "I wasn't sure I'd be able to recognize him, but that's definitely the man."

Bill closed the book and placed it in a drawer in his desk. "I'll put out an APB on him right now, Sage" he said, "But you two be careful. Lay low somewhere and try to stay out of sight."

"We'll go back to my place and stay there" I said.

"I wouldn't go back there, Sage" said Bill. "You know he can probably find you pretty easily. You might want to relocate for a while."

"Relocate? Where? Are you gonna put us in the witness protection program, Bill?"

Bill laughed slightly. "No" he said. "Just find a nice motel room somewhere as far away from your place as you can. Stay there until you hear from me."

I looked at Samantha. Neither of us thought we'd be hiding out after this little visit to the police station. "Okay" I said finally.

"Give me a call when you get settled and let me know where you are. I'll be sure to keep a cruiser in the area."

Samantha and I promised Bill we wouldn't return to my place for anything. I shook hands with Bill and as we left the police station. As we were walking to the car, I realized I would have to buy Samantha and myself some clothes. We couldn't very well wear the clothes we had on everyday for who knows how long, and although we had gone shopping for new clothes while we were playing house all week, they were back at my place.

"We're making one stop before we get to the motel" I said as we left the police station.

"For what?" she asked.

"We've got to have some clothes. We can't very well go around in the same clothes for days."

"Sure we can" she said with a devilish smile. "When they get dirty, we'll wash 'em in the bathtub."

"Oh yeah?" I asked, "And what will we wear while we're washing them?"

"Nothing" she answered.

"You've done this before" I said.

"No" she answered, "but I've always wanted to."

After Sage and Samantha had left his office, Bill Jenkins got on the phone and called Jack Marble to inform him that Maxwell Brown had just been identified as the man who'd shot the pimp in the West Bottoms.

"Damn!" said Marble. "When was this?"

"Just now. A few minutes ago. They just left my office."

"Shit" Marble said. "Well let me call his P.O. and see what she wants to do about this."

Jack hung up and called Driscoll. "We've got a problem" he said when she answered. "I just got a phone call from Bill Jenkins over at Central."

He told Driscoll the story Bill had relayed to him.

"Let me get this straight" Driscoll said. "Brown was holding a young prostitute named Trixy Bedluv for ransom?"

"Yup."

"For fifty-thousand dollars."

"Yup."

"And this Sage Chandler rode in on a white horse and saved her?"

"Yes and here's the kicker. Chandler shot the man in the left arm."

"Oh shit. And we had him. We had him until this morning."

"Yup. What do you want to do now?"

Driscoll said she'd like to have Marble meet her at the house where Max and Hughie had been living. "Bring some additional officers with you too, Jack. These guys are obviously armed."

Driscoll hung up and sat staring at the phone for several seconds. If she had held him for a revocation hearing he'd still be in custody. "Damn" she thought, "why hadn't these people come forward before now?"

She stood, put on her vest and strapped on her duty belt with the pepper spray, handcuffs and her duty weapon, a .40 caliber Glock, and left the Office. She was farther away from the West Bottoms than Marble, so she figured he'd beat her there and without a search warrant, knew Marble wouldn't enter the home without her. She'd have to drive like hell to get there in time.

Chapter 19

After leaving the police station, Hughie and Max had gone to their house in the West Bottoms and gathered their few belongings. Then they went to the Crane building to retrieve the money and guns that Hughie had stashed there. Now they were in Hughie's little car on their way to carry out their plan to bring Sage out into the open.

Hughie told Max how he'd gone to the address and set up surveillance outside the Chandler home. He'd had to wait in his car for almost two hours before anyone came outside, but the wait was worth it. The entire family had come out at once and gotten in their car and driven off together.

As they were walking from their home to their vehicle, he was able to see through his binoculars that the woman was definitely the same woman whose pictures he'd found on the Internet. "It was harder to tell if the kids were the same as the ones in my pictures," Hughie said. "They've grown up since those pictures were taken, but I'm pretty sure they are the same kids."

Hughie hadn't even bothered to follow them after they'd driven off. For one, he was satisfied that he had the right family and two, because he had to piss bad. He drove to the nearest convenience store, did his business, bought a twelve pack, and went home to wait for Max to be released from jail.

He didn't tell Max about the twelve pack because he knew Max wouldn't like his going against orders. He remembered that Max had instructed him not to get drunk, but what Max didn't know wouldn't harm Hughie.

They drove without speaking for a long time. Finally they arrived at the Chandler home. It was dark outside now. The clock on the dashboard read 9:15.

Max opened the glove box and found two handguns, a pair of .40 caliber Smith and Wesson automatics. He handed one to Hughie. "Are they hot?" he asked.

"Yeah. Locked and loaded, ready to fire."

"OK then. Let's do this."

With his Smith tucked into his pants, Hughie exited the automobile and walked to the Chandler's front door. He knocked five times. Shortly, a handsome woman came to the door.

"May I help you?" she asked.

"Could I borrow your phone?" he asked. "My car seems to have stalled and I need to call the auto club." She looked him up and down. He looked alright, she thought. He was well dressed and pretty well groomed. She looked beyond him at the car parked in front of her house. It was an older car, very small, probably a Toyota or Nissan. He seemed harmless enough.

"Sure" she said and let Hughie enter her home. She closed the door behind him. When she turned around she came face to face with the barrel of Hughie's .40 not a foot away from her face.

"Don't scream," Hughie said. "Or I'll blow your head off." She nodded in agreement. "Now, let's have a seat in your living room."

She led the way to the living room and seated herself on the couch. Hughie took a recliner facing her.

"Is this a robbery?" she asked.

"No. And don't ask questions. Are you Kim Chandler?"

She repeated what she had said on the phone, that she used to be, but was estranged from her husband. She reclaimed her maiden name after the divorce.

"But you were married to Royal Sage Chandler, the lawyer who used to work for the Higgins law firm?"

"Yes."

Hughie looked at her silently for a moment. She seemed calm and unafraid. "Is your name Kim?"

"Yes."

She may not have been afraid, but she was following his commands quite well. She wasn't asking any questions and answering his with simple answers.

"So your husband is a big time lawyer, huh?"

"Not anymore. He was let go by the firm about three years ago."

"What's he doing now?"

"I'm not really sure. He had some stupid plans a while back to become a private investigator, but I have no idea if he did it or not."

"Are your children home?"

"No."

"Where are they?"

Kim explained that her son was at a friend's house until ten and her daughter was staying overnight at one of her friend's house. "It's Friday night" she said. "Jimmy's curfew on Friday is ten."

Hughie studied her and considered her answer. "So he'll be home soon." Kim looked at her clock and realized it was much later than she thought it was.

"Yes" she said. "I expect him home within the next half hour or so."

Hughie explained to Kim that his partner was waiting in the car. "I am supposed to flip your porch light on and off again when its safe for him to enter. Do you mind flipping the light now?"

Kim did mind. Having one of these assholes in her house was enough. She didn't need another one.

"Why don't you do that yourself?"

She could tell Hughie didn't like that. His demeanor immediately changed. He glared at her momentarily.

"Lady" he began, "I will say this once. If you want you and your kids to get through this unharmed, do as I say without question because I will not hesitate to shoot you or your children."

"Okay." She stood. Hughie stood with her. She walked over and flipped the porch light off and on and returned to her place on the couch. Hughie stayed by the front door to admit Max into the house.

As Max entered, he gave the room the once over. He walked over to the couch and sat beside Kim. Hughie took up his earlier spot in the recliner.

"Hello, Miss" Max said. "We are not here to harm you, but we do intend to harm that fucker ex-husband of yours."

Hughie explained to Max that the children were out. One wouldn't be home until morning and the other would be showing up very soon. Then he told Max about Sage. "He's not a lawyer anymore, Max. Kim here doesn't know what he's doing now, but says he had a plan to become a private investigator."

"Hmmm" said Max. "That could explain why he was in the West Bottoms at 3:00 in the morning the other night."

"What's in the garage?" Max asked Kim.

"Just my car. Just my Mercedes and some other junk that has piled up over the years."

"We need to pull our car into the garage where it's out of sight for a while. Do you ever leave your car outside in the driveway?"

"Never."

"So it might seem conspicuous to the neighbors if you did."

"I doubt they'd notice... they might, but you don't have to worry about that. It's a two car garage and the other stall is empty. Sage used to park there."

"Good" Max said slyly. "Your cooperation is very much appreciate, Kim... May I call you Kim?" Without waiting for her blessing, he instructed Hughie to go check out the garage and see if she's telling the truth. "If she's tellin' the truth, pull the car into the garage, Hughie."

"Is there a direct entry from the house to the garage?" Hughie asked Kim.

"Yes. From the kitchen." She pointed in the direction of the kitchen.

"Automatic door opener?"

"Yes. The control is on the front wall to the left of the garage doors closest to the house."

Hughie scrambled out of the recliner and walked to the kitchen. He found the garage door and let himself into the garage. He found the light switch just inside the door and to his left. When the lights came on, he saw she was telling the truth. The far stall was indeed empty. He searched for the garage door control and found it exactly where Kim said it would be. He pressed the button for the right-most door and it began to open. Hughie went to his car and pulled it into the garage. He punched the button to close the door and left and reentered the house through the kitchen. As he sauntered into the living room he said "OK Boss. The car is put away. Everything was just as she said it would be."

"So far" Max said, "you are doing exactly what you should be doing; telling us the truth. Keep doing that and everyone will be fine."

Hughie resumed his seat on the recliner. "What now, Boss?"

"We wait until the son comes home" Max replied.

"Have you got anything to drink?" Max asked. Kim said she had some water, cola, or beer in the fridge. "I'd sure like one of those beers if you can spare one" Max said.

Kim went to the kitchen to retrieve the beer. Max motioned for Hughie to go with her.

"Would you like one too?" she asked Hughie reaching into the fridge.

"Sure."

She handed one beer to Hughie and carried the other back to Max. She resumed her seat on the couch. Just then, the phone rang.

"I'll get it" said a voice from somewhere."

"Who is that?" Max asked.

Kim jumped up and ran toward the kitchen where the stairway to the upstairs was. She was almost to the stairway, when Hughie grabbed her and threw her on the floor. He heard footsteps coming down the stairs. He backed away from the staircase pointing his gun at Kim. Suddenly a boy emerged.

"Mom?" he said looking concerned that his mother was lying on the floor. "What happened?"

Hughie showed the kid his pistol. "Just stay there, kid" he said. "In fact, get on the floor with your mother." Max finally came to see what was going on. When he saw the kid on the floor beside his mother, he became furious, but probably the only person who recognized his anger was Hughie. Max could control his anger when he wanted to.

"So, the kid has been here all along?" Max asked. Kim didn't answer. Max told the kid to stay on the floor. "Kim" he said, "get on your feet." She stood. He walked over close to her. She was pretty tall for a woman, only two inches short of six feet but Max still towered over her. He grabbed her by her arm. "Keep an eye on him" he said to Hughie indicating the kid.

Max escorted Kim back into the living room out of sight. He bent down and got his face very close to hers. "You lied to me, bitch" he said in a strong whisper. "You lie, you die."

He straightened and glowered and Kim. Suddenly he let her have it right in the stomach. She folded forward in pain. "Got it?" he asked.

Kim couldn't speak. He'd hit her directly in her solar plexus and knocked the wind out of her. "You better understand me." Kim nodded her head in agreement, but still couldn't speak. "Now where is your daughter?   Is she upstairs too?"

"No" Kim managed still hunched over, "At a friend's."

"When will she be home?"

"She... she's got an 11:00 curfew on weekends."

Max shouted for Hughie to bring the boy into the living room.

"We're all going to sit and have a nice visit" Max said looking at Jimmy. "We'll all just watch television until your sister gets home, son."   He directed his glance to Kim. "I suggest you play nice if you know what's good for you."

Max instructed Hughie to go upstairs and look for the daughter. "There's no reason to rely on this lying bitch" he said.   "Sit down!" he directed Kim, but she didn't move a muscle.

Max reached out and grabbed Jimmy and twisted him around so the kid's back was toward him. He reached into his pocket and produced a long switchblade knife and flipped it open. Holding it to the Jimmy's throat he said, "You will sit down, or I will cut this kid's jugular vein and he'll bleed to death right here on the floor and you won't be able to do anything but watch him die."

Kim eyed him closely. She could see he wasn't bluffing. He wasn't the type to bluff. Still he surprised her when he suddenly softened. "Listen lady" he said. "I have no reason to hurt you or your kids. If you do exactly as I say, no harm will come to any of you."

He released Jimmy and told him to put the television on and hand him the remote. Kim had studied psychology in college and had worked with violent offenders before. She knew that this crazy bastard might just kill both her and Jimmy and then wait until Lisa came home and kill her too. Kim knew she really had no other choice but to do as she was told, although it wasn't her style.

Max sat on the couch and clicked through the channels. "Not much on" he said after channel surfing for a while. "Don't you get HBO or something?" Neither Jimmy or Kim answered him.

"I like HBO" he said. "I guess I'm kind of a movie man."

Hughie returned reporting that he could find no other kids upstairs. "She's probably telling the truth about the daughter, Boss" He said.

"She is" Jimmy interjected. "My Mom doesn't lie."

Max paid the boy's comment no attention. He continued changing channels and complaining about the lack of good television viewing these days. It didn't matter much whether he found anything to watch or not. Kim and Jimmy knew it would be a long wait until Lisa got home, and then what were they in for?

Kim was thinking how she might make another break for it. If she could just get upstairs, she could get to the pistol that Sage had forced her to learn how to use. And she *had* learned how to shoot it, at least well enough to take care of these bastards if she could just get to it. She looked at the clock: 9:35.

She suddenly realized Max was watching her. She wasn't bad looking, he thought. She'd do in a pinch, even though she was much more flat-chested than the women he usually preferred. She did have a nice, small ass. He stood up and handed Jimmy the remote. He walked over close to Kim and held his hands out for her to stand up. She did, and without saying anything, Max led her to the kitchen by her arm.

"Listen" he said, "We've got an hour and a half to kill, how about a little afternoon delight?"

"No way" she said pulling away from him.

"Oh come on, Baby" he said letting go of her arm and reaching for his zipper. "Look what I've got for you."

"Whoa!" she exclaimed seeing his member. "That *is* a big one." Kim had never seen anything like it, even in some of the pornos she and Sage had watched when they were first married. This guy was literally hung like a horse. It looked like he had a summer sausage hanging between his legs.

Max smiled proudly. "Ain't it a beaut?" Kim smiled and acted as though she was interested. She took a step forward and extended her hand. As soon as Max looked down to watch her admire his monster, she turned and made a dash for the stairway. She darted up the stairs, but she was surprised at how fast Max was able to respond. He was right behind her. She thought he'd at least put that thing away before giving chase, but he hadn't bothered with that. He hadn't hesitated for one second. If he had, he wouldn't be so close behind her.

She ran as fast as she possibly could, but judging by the sound of his footsteps, Max must have been taking two steps at a time. When she reached the top of the stairs, she took a quick right turn heading for her bedroom. If she could just beat him to her nightstand, she'd have him. She didn't make it. Max caught up with her just as she reached for the nightstand drawer. He grabbed her arm and wouldn't allow her to open the drawer. She struggled in vane against his overwhelming power. He laughed.

"You must really want me bad" he said. "Seems like you couldn't wait to get up here. What have you got in the drawer, rubbers?"

He grabbed her around the waist and pulled her away from the drawer but she wouldn't let go. The drawer came all the way out spilling most of its contents on the floor. Her little pistol lay among the pictures, papers, and other junk. Max twisted her arm hard and she let go of the drawer.

"What the hell is this?" he asked reaching for the little revolver. "You were going to shoot me?"

"Damn right I'd shoot you" she spat.

Max backhanded her across the mouth, hard, then balled his fist and hit her directly in the left eye knocking her off the bed, onto the floor, and out cold. He stood and disrobed completely. Then he lifted Kim onto the bed and stripped her naked. She was still out cold, but Max didn't care. He got on top of her and tried to insert his rascal but she was too tight; too dry. She began to come around. When she realized what was happening, she screamed.

"Shut up, bitch or I'll put your lights out again."

Her left eye was beginning to swell already. Max was still trying to get started but couldn't get the monster inserted. "You better get turned on quick, bitch" he said in a low, menacing voice. "Or you better hope you got some KY in that mess beside the bed."

"I do" she said. "Reach down and get it."

Max looked her in the eye. "You better not be lying." He reached down beside the bed into the junk that had been the contents of Kim's nightstand. He rooted around and finally found a tube of something. His arm twinged and he flinched in pain as he brought the tube before his face. It was a tube of Ben Gay.

"What the hell is this?" he asked. Kim looked at the tube and hoped to hell he didn't plan on using that on her.

"That's not it" she said, "but its down there."

Max leaned over again in search of the lubricant. When he had leaned far enough, Kim suddenly got both hands on his right shoulder and pushed as hard as possible. Max began to fall, but caught himself on his left hand sending excruciating pain down his arm from his shoulder. He couldn't stand it. His arm gave out and he tumbled into a pile beside the bed among the stuff from the drawer. He was up almost immediately, but Kim was fast. She had bailed off the bed and almost made her way to the door, but Max levied another punch to her left eye and sent her sprawling backward.

"Alright bitch" he said. "I'll just drill you dry." As he approached, Kim kicked for his crotch, but missed and kicked him in the thigh. The kick infuriated Max.

"You filthy whore!' he shouted. He gathered her up and threw her back on the bed. He slapped her face hard enough to make a huge "smack" sound and leave an instant welt on her face. He then mounted her. "Put it in" he growled.

This man was hung like a horse. She knew it was going to hurt like hell but she guided him into her knowing she had no other choice. As soon as she let go, Max gave a mighty thrust and rammed it in all the way to the hilt. Kim screamed in pain. She couldn't help herself. It was more painful than she had imagined, but Max was not deterred. He put his hand over her mouth and continued with a steady, pounding rhythm. Kim found it very difficult to breath, especially with her head being knocked against the headboard with every driving thrust. She started to panic, but got control of herself.

She used her yoga techniques to calm herself as much as possible and just ride it out.

Max came like a bull. "Ugh, ugh, ugh" he grunted with each powerful thrust.

When he finished, he rolled his bulk over to the left and lay beside her, heaving. Kim lay beside him for a few seconds trying to catch her breath too.

"Mind if I clean myself up?" she asked finally.

"By all means" he breathed, "clean yourself up, you filthy whore."

She rolled over and Max slapped her backside hard. "Nice can" he said laughing.

Kim went into the adjacent bathroom. There was no way she could escape. The only entrance to the bathroom was through the bedroom right past Max.

His shoulder hurt. He examined it. It wasn't bleeding but it sure as hell was sore. He got off the bed and dressed. "Hurry up in there" he shouted. "You're clean enough for where you're going."

She emerged from the bathroom wearing a towel to cover her nudity. As she passed him, he jerked the towel away.

"Let me get a look at what I just had." he said. She tried to pass him and find her clothes, but he stopped her and pushed her backward. "Stand there a minute" he growled.

Her left eye was swelling bad now. "Damn" he said. "You have a pretty tight little body. Sorry about the eye, but it's your own fault."

She stood there allowing him to ogle her. Finally he tired of his little intimidation game. "Okay" he said. "Put your clothes on now."

She dressed and they left the bedroom. Kim was in the lead with Max holding her little revolver in his huge hand, barrel embedded in Kim's back. They descended the stairs and reentered the kitchen. When they reached the living room, Jimmy screamed at the sight of his mother's beaten face.

"Mom!" he said leaping to his feet and running to her and hugging her. "What did he do to you, Mom?"

Kim held him close to her and tried to keep him calm. "It's alright" she whispered. "I am all right. Don't worry, honey, it will all be okay." She glanced at the clock. It was two minutes to ten. "That didn't take long" she thought.

"Now then," Max sighed as he resumed his place on the couch. "Is there anything on TV now, Jimmy?"

Everyone sat down and watched Max's uneasy channel surfing. He didn't stay on any one channel long enough to really see what was on. He had an immediate and nasty comment for everyone who appeared on the screen.

"Commie" he said, when Larry King appeared. Next channel. "Prick" he said to Jerry Seinfeld. "Smiling asshole" he said to whoever the senator who was speaking on C-SPAN2. He continued that way channel after channel. Kim thought this was the way this sick bastard watched TV. He'd just cruise the channels and call everyone names.

"Got any more beer?" he asked. Kim stood to go to the kitchen to retrieve another beer. Her left eye had swollen completely shut by then, and a nasty bruise was well on its way to forming. She was gonna have a hell of a shiner for a while.

"Hold on" Hughie shouted knowing Max wouldn't want her going to the kitchen alone. He stood and followed Kim to the kitchen. She reached into the fridge and pulled out two cans of beer. Hughie said "Maybe you should put some ice on that eye."

Kim disregarded his suggestion and handed him one of the cans. "Drink up" she said. "In fact, I think I'll have one too." She turned and floundered in the fridge until she came up with another can of beer. She shut the fridge door and popped the can open.

"I'm sorry about Max" Hughie said in a low voice. "He can be... rough sometimes."

"Rough?" Kim said. "He's a fucking monster."

"Yeah."

Kim walked past Hughie and lead the way back to the living room. She handed the unopened can of beer to Max.

"Thank you" he said and popped the top. "Now we wait. It shouldn't be much longer now."

They sat quietly and resumed watching Max channel surf and cuss at everyone who appeared. He seemed to hate everyone. He had nothing good to say about anyone. Even the pretty girls on the workout shows weren't above ridicule. "I'd fuck her" he'd say. "How about you Hughie?"

Hughie would agree with Max, whatever he said. He knew he was expendable in Max's eyes. Everyone was. Hughie knew that Max wouldn't hesitate to beat him to a bloody pulp or even kill him if he ever disagreed.

Kim was appalled at Max's behavior. "Please" she objected, "watch the language in front of my son."

Max glared at her for a second. "Shut the fuck up, bitch", he said or I'll fuck you again right here in front of your son... This time in the ass. How do you suppose that would be?" Kim had no response. She didn't want to provoke this bastard, but that statement made her wonder if any of them would get out of this alive. She seriously doubted that they would.

Jimmy didn't know exactly what Max was talking about but if 'fuck' meant Mom would end up with another black eye, then he knew he didn't want that. He snuggled closer to Kim and hugged her tightly. "Don't worry Mom" he said, "He's not going to fuck you in the eye again."

Kim looked down at her son. "Oh goody" she thought. "Now he's repeating the 'F' word." She wondered if he had any idea what he'd just said. She couldn't correct him, or explain why he shouldn't use words like that. They'd just have to tough this out somehow. She'd worry about how to deal with whatever bad language Jimmy had picked up later. Right now, it was all about surviving this situation.

She and Jimmy sat together in a large rocking recliner. They remained as quiet as possible. She hated that Jimmy was being subjected to Max's horrible language, but it absolutely couldn't be helped. She did not doubt for a minute that Max would rape her again right in front of Jimmy and she couldn't think of anything worse than that. God she hoped he wouldn't rape Lisa. She was a pretty girl, but she was only a girl. She prayed that this bastard wasn't into little girls.

Time passed slowly as they waited for Lisa to arrive. They quietly tolerated Max's foul language for about twenty minutes. Suddenly about 10:35 they heard someone on the porch.

"Nobody move" Max whispered. "And stay quiet."

As Lisa entered the room she said, "Hi Mom. I'm home a little early." Hughie jumped up gun in hand pointed directly at Lisa. "Don't move" he said. Lisa had been removing her coat. She froze midstream. The only light in the house was coming from the television. Her eyes had not yet adjusted to the dimly lit room, but she could see well enough to know there was a gun pointed at her.

"What's going on?" she asked.

"Don't talk" Hughie said. "Just take your coat off and join the others in the living room."

Max sat up and turned his head in Lisa's direction. "Yeah" he said with a huge smile. "Come join us. Lets see what you look like."

Kim was beginning to panic again. Her worst nightmare might actually come true tonight. She might have to watch as her daughter is raped and murdered before her eyes.

"Come on honey" she said noticing the trembling of her own voice. "Come sit by Jimmy and me." As Lisa approached her mother, she became aware of the damage that had been inflicted on Kim's face.

"Mom" she exclaimed. "What happened?" She began to cry and went and sat beside her mother on the couch burying her face between Kim's breasts.

"What did you do to her?" she shouted suddenly, her anger directed at Max.

"Shh" Max said calmly, and then drained his beer. "Stand up. Let me take a look at you." Lisa looked at Kim for advice. Kim nodded. "Stand up, dear. Its alright." Lisa stood.

"Turn around" Max commanded. As Lisa turned Max gave her a good once over. She was a pretty girl, with long, thick, dark hair, dark eyes, about five feet five inches tall. Very shapely for her age.

"What do ya think, Hughie?" Max asked. "She's ripening up pretty nice, wouldn't you say?"

Hughie agreed as always. Max stared at Lisa a while longer. "Yup" he said suddenly switching his glance to Kim. "Very pretty girl, indeed" he said, with a wink of an eye. The warning wasn't wasted on Kim. She understood what Max meant well enough.

"We'll give you no trouble" she said.

"Good" he answered. "We're all gonna leave now, and if no one causes me any problems, you will not be harmed. Mom got the shiner because she tried to fight me. Don't do that, and everything will be fine."

He stood and Lisa remarked at how huge the guy was. He was the biggest man she'd ever seen up close.

"Let's go now."

Chapter 20

As she entered the West Bottoms, Driscoll radioed Marble. "What's your twenty, over?" she said.

"About two blocks from the destination" Marble answered.

"Been here long, over?"

"Not long. Where are you?"

Driscoll noticed that Marble didn't use standard radio protocol. He didn't use the codes or say "over" after every transmission. She wondered why. Then she wondered why she wondered.

"I am almost to the destination, over."

"We are standing by waiting for your arrival... Detective Marble out."

Driscoll drove a while longer and then spotted a black Ford Crown Victoria parked up the street on the right. She pulled in behind and Marble got in her passenger side.

"The little car that was here is gone." Marble explained. "What do you want to do?"

"Let's go in and see if they are here. I doubt they will be, but it's the best place to start our search."

They exited the car, and with the officers behind them, walked the short distance to the house where Max and Hughie had been living. With her gun drawn, Driscoll knocked on the door. No answer. She knocked again. No answer. She tried the door. It was unlocked. It swung open very easily.

"Doesn't even have a lock" Driscoll said after examining the door. "Either they have nothing of any value here, or one or the other of them was always home."

They cautiously entered the domicile. Marble first, then the other officers, and finally Driscoll bringing up the rear.

"Police!" Marble yelled, but got no response. They quickly checked the other rooms. They were all empty. The laptop computer, the cooler in the kitchen, everything had been removed.

"They're on the move" Marble said.

"Yes but to where? They could be out of the city by now."

"Let's get back to the car and radio in an APB."

They left the old home and walked briskly back to their cars. Marble radioed Central Dispatch. "We need an APB on a late 1990s model Nissan Sentra, blue in color. License unknown, but It may be registered to one Hughie Long."

As Marble, Driscoll, and the officers sat in Marble's Crown Vic discussing what they should do next, the APB came over the radio.

"There we go" Marble said. "Now we wait to see if anyone reports anything." In the meanwhile they decided to check out the Crane building where the pimp had been shot. It was unlikely, but they could have taken refuge there, or perhaps left a clue. Hopefully by the time they finished their search, someone would have spotted the blue Nissan.

As they drove toward the Crane building, Dricoll was looking around at the ruins that were the West Bottoms.

"Pretty ugly, huh?" Marble asked. Ugly wasn't the word that Driscoll would have used to describe this place. It was the shittiest place she'd ever seen and she'd seen some shitty neighborhoods in her time, but his place definitely took the cake.

They drove around the neighborhood looking for the Crane building, or better yet, an older blue Nissan Sentra. They found the Crane building first. Marble parked the car and all four officers got out and walked to the front doors of the building.

"This is where the pimp found his reward" Marble said.

"And look up here" Driscoll said ascending the stairs. "Look at the blood stains here by the door. That must be where Max was standing when this Chandler character shot him."

"Must be" Marble agreed.

They noticed the front doors were locked, but it didn't matter much because both doors were framed in glass, and one had been broken out almost completely.

"Well" Marble said, "lets go see what we can find."

Marble led the way. He carefully ducked through the door with the broken glass followed by the other two police officers. Driscoll went through last with the uniformed officers supervising. "Whatever happened to 'Ladies First'?" she muttered. If anyone heard her, they didn't respond.

Inside was another building in ruins. There were holes in the walls and old wallpaper had torn away and was hanging raggedly from the walls. Pieces of wood and plaster were lying all over the floor. Even in this condition, Driscoll could tell that master craftsmen had built this place. Rotted oak floors covered in dust that led to staircases with carved oak banisters. The stairs themselves were marble, now chipped and broken.

"This must have been some showplace seventy five years ago" she said. "It's a real shame to let historic buildings like this end up as abandoned ruins."

They searched the four floors of the Crane Building one by one and found nothing. They searched the basement and found nothing but a doorway that led to a concrete staircase that led up to the street.

"Look" Marble said. "More blood stains."

"Could be from Max" Driscoll said. "Sure as hell wasn't from the pimp."

"Yeah, but that blood could be from anyone." Marble knelt down to examine the stain more closely.

"Don't touch it without your gloves" Driscoll warned.

Marble ignored her. "No way to tell without matching it to Max's blood" he said. "It very well might be Max's, but it doesn't really matter anyway. We already know Max was shot here."

They decided the Crane building held no further clues. Max and Hughie weren't here unless they were holed up in some secret passageway Driscoll and Marble hadn't found yet. They elected to return to the vehicle and see if the APB had turned anything.

"Where the hell would Max go?" Driscoll asked walking to the car. "I wish I had a better handle on Max's psyche."

"Yeah..." Marble responded not really paying attention.

They got in the black Crown Vic and radioed dispatch to see if there was any news. Some vehicles matching the description of Hughie's Nissan had been stopped but none of the VIN numbers matched.

Driscoll and Marble sat without speaking for a few moments. Both were trying to understand what they would do in Max's position.

"Do you think there's any chance Max knows who shot him?" Driscoll asked.

"How could he?"

"I don't know, but if he did know, he seems like the kind of guy who would want revenge."

"Oh definitely."

"So how would he exact his revenge? What types of crimes has he committed?" She thought about her question. "Or even been suspected of?" she added before Marble could answer.

"Not sure" Marble said. "Let's find out." Marble grabbed the microphone and called dispatch for a description of Max's rap sheet. Driscoll listened intently to the results: burglary, robbery, rape, kidnapping, assault, and murder.

"Kidnapping" she said. "That's it. We know that he kidnapped a prostitute for ransom from the pimp, right?"

"Yeah, that's what Jenkins said."

"Where was he holding her?"

"That I don't know, but I can find out."

Marble pulled out his cell phone and Called the Central Division. "Bill Jenkins, please."

Marble was informed that Jenkins had left for the day and wouldn't be back until the next day at 8:00 am. He asked for Jenkins's personal phone number, but the dispatcher informed him that his personal phone number was unlisted and she could not give out that information under any circumstances.

"My name is Detective Jack Marble, from the Western Division. You want my badge number?"

"No sir, I still cannot give out personal information over the phone. I'm sorry."

"But this is important! People's lives are at stake. Do you want to be responsible for people's lives?"

"No sir. I am just following departmental procedures, sir."

Marble could see he would never get this woman to violate departmental procedures. "Can you relay a message to Detective Jenkins?"

"Yes sir."

Marble told her to call Jenkins and ask him where Maxwell Brown had held the prostitute he'd kidnapped. "I need the name of the building, the exact location. Got it?"

"Yes sir, right away, sir."

Marble gave the dispatcher his cell phone number, although he doubted he needed to; she probably already had it. "Can you do something else for me?"

"I'll try, sir."

"Can you give me an address on one Sage Chandler? He was once a high profile attorney who was employed for the Higgins Law Firm."

"Certainly."

Marble waited while the dispatcher looked up the information.

"God Damn procedures" he said to Driscoll. She did not answer.

The dispatcher came back to the phone. "Detective Marble?"

"Yes, I'm still here."

"Sir, that address is 810 Grand Elm Street."

Marble thanked her and snapped his cell phone shut. "Damn" he said. "That address is on the other side of town. It'll take us a while to get there."

"Well" said Driscoll, "its the only lead we have right now until you hear from Jenkins."

Marble grabbed the microphone and called dispatch again and instructed the dispatcher to send the closest cruiser to 810 Grand Elm Street. "There's a possible kidnapping in progress."

Almost instantly the request came over the radio. "All cars in the vicinity of 810 Grand Elm Street please report to that location ASAP."

Seconds later the radio came alive with cruisers in the area. Several cars were on their way to the Chandler home. Driscoll and Marble could only wait for a report.   They decided to remain in the West Bottoms area and cruise around looking for anything suspicious.

Chapter 21

After leaving the Police Station, Samantha and I stopped at a shopping center to purchase new clothes, before continuing to the Plaza. There were several nice hotels in the Plaza and we decided if we were going on vacation, we might as well stay somewhere nice. We were certain we'd find a hotel to our liking. As we drove along suddenly Samantha said, "Hey Sage, look!" I whipped my head toward her but she was pointing at something out my window. I followed her finger. She was pointing at a billboard that read, "Live Music – Mon – Sat. 9:00 to Close. And before I could read it Samantha shouted.

"Jimmy Wakefield and the Hustlers!"

"Who are they?" I asked.

"Haven't you heard them?" she asked. "They play the traditional country music we both like. I heard 'em once in a club downtown. They're good."

I turned into the parking lot of the Sheraton Suites Hotel. "I guess this is as good a place as any" I said, "At least they have live music and a bar."

Samantha was excited about seeing this band again. She must have really liked them. We parked under the canopy, entered the hotel, and approached the front desk.

"We'd like a room for the night, please?" Samantha asked before I could. "One with a whirlpool tub, if possible."

"Certainly" replied the pretty, young lady behind the counter. She was tall and blond about 22 years old give or take a year. She was very pleasant and very professional in her appearance and behavior.

We checked signed the register. Since I didn't want to use my real name, Samantha suggested that we sign is as Mr. and Mrs. "Floyd Johnson." Floyd was Samantha's uncle. If she had to provide a first name, she figured she could just use her real name. She concluded that other than Detective Jenkins, Papa, and me, no one had ever known her true identity, so we might as well use it as an alias. So for the time being were Mr. and Mrs. Floyd Johnson. Sounded good to me.

"Here you go" said the young, blond, blue-eyed desk clerk. "You're in room 213." She showed us where to park and the door closest to our room. "Have a nice stay" she said as we turned to leave.

We got back in the car and drove around to our entrance. We had no luggage, but we did have the bags of clothing we'd purchased en route to the hotel. We took the stairs to our room. It was only one flight up on the second floor. Neither of us were overly interested in exercise, but we figured we could manage one flight of stairs.

The room was nice for a hotel room. It was somewhat bigger than many of the hotel rooms I'd stayed in. Once nice aspect was that the whirlpool tub was not in the bathroom, but in a little nook between the bathroom and the bedroom. I was glad that Samantha had thought to ask for a Jacuzzi tub, because now it looked very inviting. It was large enough for two people, and had eight jets per person.

"Oh boy" Samantha said, "That looks good." I agreed. I could hardly wait to get in and let the stress bubble away.

"I'm going to change," Samantha said suddenly. "I want to get something to eat. I'm starving."

"Yeah" I said, suddenly realizing I was hungry too. "Let's go downstairs to the restaurant and eat, and then we'll buy a bottle of wine and come back to the tub here."

"Sounds great" she said, "but let's make it two bottles... and bubbles too. I like to put bath bubbles in the whirlpool." I didn't much care if we had bubbles or not, but the idea of two bottles did sound better than one.

Samantha changed into one of her new outfits, simple blue jeans, a pink pull over shirt with three buttons in front, and a pair of Nike sneakers. She reapplied her makeup, and was ready to go all in about ten minutes.

We walked the short distance down the stairs to the front desk and asked the tall, blond desk clerk where the restaurant was. She pointed us in the general direction.

"Is there a liquor store hereabouts?" I asked.

"Yes sir, there is" she answered. "You will pass it on your way to the restaurant. It's in the back of the lounge."

"Good enough" I replied and we meandered toward the restaurant noticing the liquor store and lounge on our way. It was only a short distance further and we entered the Sheraton Le Plaza Restaurant. We waited only a short while by the sign that read "Please Wait to be Seated." Soon a middle-aged woman came and led us to a small table for two in the back, near a window. "A waitress will be right with you" she said as she scurried away.

We sat across from each other at the small table. The atmosphere was nice. It was somewhat dark even though it was only early afternoon. The silk flowers and short, stocky candle on our table helped set a mood. The candle smelled of something I couldn't identify.

"Lilacs" Samantha said. "Like it?"

"Yeah" I said, "its kind of nice."

We chatted about the ambiance of the place and looked at the rows of bottles of wines on the wall beside us. We checked out the drinks and desserts on the table tents that were on the tables. "I am just starving" Samantha said.

Just then a waitress appeared carrying two glasses of ice water with a lemon wedge in each, and two menus. We opened the menus and began browsing.

"What are you hungry for?" I asked.

"Not sure yet" Samantha said, "I'm kind of on the fence between the taco salad and a cheeseburger."

"Oh" I said, "Where'd you see the taco salad?"

She reached across the table to my menu, turned the page, and pointed to the taco salad.

"Thank you." I couldn't help but smile at her. She returned my smile with a sort of embarrassed look.

"That looks good to me" I said, "and a Corona to go with it."

Samantha continued studying her menu for a few more seconds. "I think I'll have the chicken salad with bread sticks." she said finally. I didn't know why she'd changed her mind about the taco salad, but it sounded really good to me.

When the waitress returned, we ordered and the waitress was off to retrieve our drinks. My Corona arrived with its wedge of lime which I squeezed into the bottle. I didn't really care for Corona unless I was eating a Mexican-type dish. Samantha ordered a diet soda with a twist of lemon.

As we waited for our food, we continued talking about this and that and nothing in particular. I told her that I really enjoyed her company and that she was fun to be with. I hadn't felt this way in a long time.

"I feel the same way, Sage" she said. "I think I am falling hard for you."

I smiled at that. I was falling for her too, and I wanted to tell her so, but for some reason, I wanted to wait a few more days.

"All we gotta do" I said, "is get past this little situation and then we can be together."

"Yeah" she said, "That reminds me. What were you and Detective Jenkins talking about when you left his office?"

I told her about our conversation, leaving out the worst parts about what a badass this Maxwell Brown is. Besides, she knew firsthand what a bastard he was.

"He didn't care that you shot him?" she asked.

"Didn't seem to" I answered. "In fact he said he wished I'd shot him dead."

We chatted a bit more about what we would do after Jenkins and his boys had apprehended Brown. We talked about how long it would take them to find him and what we'd do if we had to stay in this hotel for more than a week.

"We might have to move to another hotel" Samantha said.

"I doubt it" I said, "Jenkins is pretty good. He'll round Brown up before too long."

"I hope so, Sage. I don't mind staying here for a few days. It'll be like a vacation, but I'm a home body. I want to go back to your place pretty soon."

"I know, honey" I said. "Me too."

We sat quietly staring into each other's eyes and smiling our asses off for a half-minute or so. "Tell me about your kids" she said finally, "what are their names?"

"Lisa and James" I replied, "Lisa is fifteen and James is ten."

"I can't wait to meet them" she said.

Just then I remembered I was supposed to call Jenkins and let him know where we were. I took out my cell phone and dialed the number for the Central Division.

"Detective Jenkins, please" I said.

Bill came on the phone and I gave him the information. "Oh" he said, "that's a nice place to hole up for a while. I'll make sure a cruiser comes by every half hour looking for anyone fitting Brown's description. You just hunker down with that little girl and relax."

I assured him that I intended to do just that. He hung up and I turned my attention to Samantha.

Soon our meals arrived and we ate in relaxation. My taco salad was quite good, one of the best I'd ever had. I wasn't sure if it really was that good, or if it was the overall ambiance and being there with Samantha, but it was really tasty.

After we finished eating, we paid the bill, left a generous tip, and walked to the liquor store in the rear of the lounge to pick up our wine. After shopping for a few minutes, we picked out a couple of nice wines. I found a Shiraz I wanted to try and Samantha found a White Merlot she thought we'd like.

We returned to our room, Samantha went to the bathroom. I looked around for a corkscrew but wasn't really surprised when I didn't find one. All was not lost, however because being and old Boy Scout, I believe in being prepared. I suddenly remembered my Swiss Army Knife would be equipped with a cork screw. I opened the White Merlot and filled two plastic glasses with the wonderful grape juice, then I began drawing a bath in the whirlpool.

"Damn" Samantha shouted through the bathroom door a moment after I'd started the bath, "We didn't get any bubbles."

"Yeah," I said, "I guess we forgot."

Samantha emerged from the bathroom totally nude carrying two bath towels still folded as the maid had left them. "You still dressed?" she asked. She set the towels beside the tub. She looked so good standing there naked with her "after-market hooters" as Papa had called them and her nicely trimmed, reddish-blond patch.

"Was Papa into hot rods?" I asked.

"What?"

"Never mind." I grabbed her and pulled her toward me. I kissed her hard and then I bent down and got an arm behind her knees and swooped her off her feet and carried her to the bed. When I set her on the bed, she scrambled under the covers while I ripped my clothes off and scattered them all over the room. We made love. It was the best I've ever had.

Afterward we lay there heaving. "That was spontaneous" she said.

"I couldn't help it."

"Oh don't apologize. I liked it."

I climbed under the covers and we snuggled for a while. We both fell asleep. We awoke in pitch dark. I looked at the digital clock beside the bed. It read 10:57. Where had the time gone? I looked over at Samantha. She was waking up too.

"We've been in bed for like six hours" I said.

"I guess we needed the sleep" she said.

After a few minutes, she got out of bed and walked to the whirlpool and tested the water with her foot. "Could be hotter" she said.

I laughed heartily. "No shit?"

She drained the tub and refilled it with hot water. While the tub was filling she poured us each a glass of wine. "Nothing like warm wine in plastic cups" she said. "Man, that's my idea of high living."

When the tub had filled Samantha climbed in. "Ahhh" she sighed. "That is nice."

I got up and joined her in the tub. She handed me a glass of wine. It was one of those tubs where two people sit opposite one another. When I realized I had access to Samantha's feet, I set my glass on the edge of the tub and began rubbing her feet under water.

She moaned and laid her head on the back of the tub, sipping her wine from time to time. We lay that way for a long time not talking, just letting the jets work their magic on our backs, and legs refilling our glasses now and then. It was marvelous. After we had almost finished the first bottle of wine, I was beginning to feel like a lobster.

"I gotta get out" I said. Samantha didn't answer, just sort of nodded in acknowledgement.

I got out, toweled off, and made my way to the bed. My legs would barely hold me up. I was hot; in fact, I was spent. Hot tubs always do that to me. I lay there on the bed for a few minutes my muscles so relaxed they felt like rubber. I must have dozed off for a short time because I was startled by my cell phone going off. I rolled off the bed and crawled on the floor to where my shirt lay. I found my phone in the shirt pocket and answered without looking at the number.

"Dad?" the voice on the other end asked. For a split second I didn't recognize the voice. Then I did.

"Jimmy?" I asked.

"Yeah Dad" he said, it's me and I don't know where I am..." Suddenly another voice came on the phone. "Well,

well" he said, "Mr. Chandler. We talk again." My heart sank as I realized who I was talking to and what the ramifications of this call could mean.

"Yes" I managed before being cut off.

"Have you come to terms yet with the fact that I have your son, Mr. Chandler?"

"Why do you have my son?"

"Shut up!" he commanded. "Don't talk, just listen... I have your son and you have eight hours to come get him."

I looked at the clock on the wall above the television. It was 12:15 am. I didn't say anything as I'd been instructed. I didn't want to do anything to put Jimmy in more danger.

"If you haven't found him after the eight hours have expired... well, you know what will happen, Mr. Chandler."

"Why?" I asked. Then there was some ruckus on the phone. "There, now we can talk more candidly."

"What did you do?"

"We just took your son away so he can't hear our conversation, that's all." Samantha sat up in the bathtub looking at me with concern. "What?" she mouthed. I held up my right hand to tell her to wait. She sat there silently.

"We're gonna kill your son if you don't find him in eight hours, Mr. Chandler."

"Why?" I asked again.

"Because you shot me in the arm, and I want to pay you back for that."

"By killing my son?"

"No, Mr. Chandler, by killing you." A pause. "If you can find us in eight hours, I will turn your son lose in exchange for your life. You have my word."

I waited to see what he would say next, but he just remained silent. Finally, I felt like I had no choice but to ask. "And if I don't find you in eight hours?"

"Well, Mr. Chandler, your son's life will be cut short."

"You son of a bitch" I blurted, immediately wishing I hadn't. "Just tell me where you are. My son has done nothing to you."

"I know he hasn't, and he's a good-looking kid. Be a shame to waist him, but I will, Mr. Chandler. Believe me, I will."

"All right, all right" I said, "give me a clue as to where you are holding him, and I'm on my way."

Max laughed like he'd just been told the best joke he'd ever heard. "That shouldn't be hard for a smart guy like you to figure out, Mr. Chandler. I am pretty close to where I was the night you shot me."

"So you are in the West Bottoms somewhere?"

Max didn't answer immediately. I figured he was trying to create tension. "Mr. Chandler" he said finally, "Your son is only the beginning. Once your son is dead I will give you another eight hours to find us or I will kill your daughter."

"You have my daughter too?"

"Yes, I do" he said, "and your ex-wife."

"But I am the one you want. Why not just let me know where you are and I'll come there and we can have this out."

"Oh Mr. Chandler" he said, "That would take all the excitement out of this for both of us. It will be much more fun my way... you'll see. Do not call the cops, Mr. Chandler. If I see anything that even remotely resembles a cop, you can kiss your whole family goodbye. And don't bring anyone else with you either, unless that little whore is still with you. She owes me a free one... Better start soon, Mr. Chandler... the clock starts now." The call ended. I snapped my phone shut.

"What?" Samantha asked impatiently.

"He's got my son."

"What?"

"Maxwell Brown... He's got my son. He also claims to have my daughter and Kim, but I didn't talk to them so I am not sure. He may be bluffing. I opened my phone and dialed Kim's number. No answer. I decided to leave a message in case she was just out. I waited for her voice mail. "Hey this is Kim. Leave a message after the beep."

Beep. "Kim" I began, "It's me. Give me a call when you get this. It's really important." I hung up and looked at Samantha. She had pulled the plug in the tub and was standing up toweling off. "What are we going to do?" she asked.

"I have eight hours to find them or my son is dead." I checked the clock again. It was almost 12:30 already. "That gives me until 8:30 to find them.

"I'm coming with." she said.

"No" I demanded, "it will be dangerous. I don't want anything happening to you."

"Fuck that, Sage" she said, "We're a team. If you're in trouble, I'm in trouble. I'm coming with!" She reminded me of her competency with handguns and I suddenly realized I hadn't brought the .40 with me. "OK" I said, "but we'll have to hurry back to my place to get the .40s."

"Well" she began, "Let's get packed up and get out of here so we don't have to lose any more time than necessary."

"Yeah" I agreed getting up to find my clothes. "I guess the honeymoon is over."

Chapter 22

We packed up and raced out of the Hotel not bothering to check out. They had our credit card number. We hadn't made any phone calls, so we didn't owe them anything. Hell, we left them a fine bottle of Shiraz as a tip.

We threw our belongings in the car, climbed in and stormed off driving as fast as I dared for home, dodging in and out of traffic. Samantha was holding on for dear life. We spoke very little during the drive. I was doing my best Jeff Gordon impersonation. Samantha didn't want to distract me with conversation. I suddenly remembered someone I'd heard about, someone who might be able to help us. "I know a guy" I said when we'd gotten into slower traffic.

"What guy?" Samantha asked.

I told her about a guy I'd heard about when I was an attorney who could take care of things like this. "His name is Sam Reynolds, but people who know him call him *Blackie*. He is what is called a cleanup man."

"A cleanup man?" She asked.

"Yeah. A cleanup man is kind of a bad guy for the good guys. Sometimes good guys get into trouble too". I explained that cops and lawyers sometimes do stupid things like get caught with hookers, or get in fights and someone winds up badly hurt or even killed.

Sometimes cops shoot the wrong people. Other times a con will come after the lawyer or cop who he blames for putting him in jail. "Fucking criminals think that way" I said. "It's always someone else's fault."

I took a sharp left turn suddenly, throwing Samantha against the car door.

"Christ Sage" she said.

"Anyway" I continued, "the point is, Sam Reynolds is a cleanup man and I think that's what we need right now."

The trouble was, I didn't know how to get hold of the guy. I thought maybe I could call Bill Jenkins, but then Bill would ask questions. On the other hand, Bill owed me a favor from the old days. Maybe this was a good time to call in my markers. Besides, I couldn't think of anyone else I could trust.

When we got to the house, I found the .40s and told Samantha where to find the ammo. While she searched, I called Jenkins. I guessed Samantha would be very surprised and happy to find that I had a good supply of ammunition for both weapons.

She emerged from the bedroom into the kitchen where I was on the phone with Jenkins. She set a backpack on the kitchen table.

"I need you to not ask any questions, Bill, and just tell me how to get in touch with Sam Reynolds."

"Sam Reynolds!" Bill shouted so loud Samantha heard him over my phone. "Blackie Reynolds? What do you want with him?"

"No questions, Bill, remember? Just suffice it to say that I need something cleaned up"

"I phoned Marble and told him your story" Jenkins said. "There's an APB on Maxwell Brown right now. Let the police handle it."

"Please Bill. Just give me the number."

"What are you getting yourself into, Sage? You're not going to mess around with Maxwell Brown, are you?"

"Bill" I said in a voice that surprised me, "If you ever trusted me, then trust me now." Jenkins finally agreed and I finally began writing down the information on Sam Reynolds. Bill had a phone number but he didn't think it would be a good idea to call Blackie at that time of night.

"I know it's late" I said, "but I have to get in touch with him now." I jotted down the number, thanked Bill and hung up.

"Bill doesn't think I should call this guy now" I said. "But what choice do I really have?" I dialed the number and waited for an answer. When someone answered I said, "Hello? Is this Sam Reynolds?"

I introduced myself and of course he asked if I was the was the same Sage Chandler who had been a high profile attorney, but no more. I told him that I was the same Sage Chandler and began to give a synopsis of the situation. He suddenly stopped me. He didn't want to talk about this on the phone. He gave me an address where he would be for the next couple of hours.

"OK" I said. "We'll be there."

"What did he say?" Samantha asked.

"I have the address of a place where Reynolds hangs out. He said we should meet him there now."

"He didn't seem to mind me calling so late" I added.

"That's good."

She walked over to the table and slapped the backpack. She said "I grabbed all the ammo, both guns and stuffed it in this backpack I found in the bottom of your closet."

"Come on then" I said.

"Where we going?"

Without answering, I grabbed Samantha's hand and pulled her though the house. She was barely able to grab the backpack off the kitchen table on the way by.

We flew into the car, and peeled out. I was driving fast again. "Sage!" Samantha shouted.

I looked over at her. "What?" I asked, half annoyed.

"Where are we going?"

"We're going to an after-hours place called the Empire Room on east Thirty-First Street. Know the place?"

"No. Never heard of it."

"Me neither."

So we drove like hell through town. I know my way around like a Cabdriver. I know back streets and short cuts like the back of my hand. Samantha had never been the places we were going now. Of course, she hadn't really been that many places in this city or lived here that long. I had twenty-some years experience driving around this city.

When we finally turned onto Thirty-First Street, it was about 1:30 am. It had been an hour since we left the hotel. We were actually making pretty good time.

"Reynolds said he hangs out at this Empire Room every night except Sundays." I said. "He's usually there earlier, but he said he's a night owl and agreed to meet us there."

Suddenly we flew past the Empire Room finding no place to park. Two blocks up the street was a parking garage. I whipped into the garage and up to the attendant's gate for a ticket. We parked and ran toward the exit of the garage. We emerged on Thirty-First Street and began walking toward the Empire Room. I was walking fast. Samantha was having a hard time keeping up.

It was almost quarter to seven when we opened the door to the Empire Room. Inside it was dark. Two piano players were dueling it out playing some kind of bluesy number. Sage had never actually met Sam Reynolds. He knew him only by reputation. He walked toward the bar and asked the bartender if he'd seen Sam lately.

"Why are you looking for Blackie?" he asked. "You a cop?"

"A lawyer" Sage answered.

The bartender pointed to a man sitting in the darkest corner of the bar. I couldn't see him well enough to make out any details, but I could see he was kicked back in his chair enjoying the music. He was wearing a cowboy hat low over his eyes.

Sage ordered two beers and we stayed by the bar waiting for our eyes to adjust to the darkness. I took a big slug of beer. "Are you ready?" I asked Samantha.

"Let's do it" she answered.

We walked in tandem toward the man seated at the table in the dark corner of the barroom. As we approached him, he showed no sign of concern. Now that my eyes had adjusted, I could see he was dressed completely in black. His clothes were black, his hat was black, even his cowboy boots were black. He had a dark full beard that provided a home for his eyes. His gray-streaked mustache was huge. It covered his entire mouth and curled a bit at the ends sticking out past his face. I walked up and stood in front of him. The man didn't move, didn't even look up.

"Are you Sam Reynolds?" I asked.

"Excuse me," the man said, "but you are blocking my view." A big smile came across his face and I could actually see his teeth through the huge mustache.

"Please" he said. "Have a seat." We sat down and I introduced Samantha and myself. We shook hands and greeted each other.

"Sage Chandler" the man said leaning back in his chair. "It's a pleasure." He lit a cigar and took a swig of his beer. "I remember you were developing a very successful career some years back and suddenly dropped out of sight." He smiled again. "I've done work for Higgins in the past myself." He went silent again while he swigged his beer and puffed his cigar.

"I know that" I said. "That's how I remembered your name."

The man considered that for a few seconds like he was remembering something pleasant.

"And In whose employ do you currently find yourself, Mr. Chandler?"

"Please, just call me 'Sage'. I am no longer an attorney. I'm a private investigator now."

"Wait" Reynolds said interrupting me. "This is my favorite part."

"Favorite part?" I wondered what he was talking about. Has he worked with many attorneys turned private investigator or what? Eventually I realized he was referring to the music the two pianos were playing. Samantha and I listened to the music obligatorily for a short time waiting for Reynolds to signal us that it was safe to speak again.

"Isn't it interesting?" Reynolds said. "How the pianos are in harmony, yet seem to be at odds with one another at the same time?"

"Ah" I began, "I really don't know that much about music."

"Well you should educate yourself" replied Reynolds. "Music is the art of the truly enlightened."

"So" I spoke carefully, "can you help us or not?"

"That Depends" Reynolds said. "You were referred you to me by whom?"

"Detective Bill Jenkins."

"Oh you are friendly with Bill" Reynolds said more as a statement than a question. Leaning forward and resting his arms on the table he said, "Bill's a good man. I've worked with Bill on several occasions... OK, if you're a friend of Bill's, I believe we can do business. Do you know who is holding your family?"

"A man named Maxwell Brown." Reynolds nodded as he sipped his beer. "I know him." he said. "He is a filthy piece of trash, of less value than a common housefly, but if he said he'll kill your family, you can believe it. The man is a scoundrel first rate. Have you any idea where he's holding them?"

"I'm pretty certain." I told him the whole story about Brown kidnapping Samantha and holding her for ransom. How he'd shot Papa, the whole story.

"And you were being held in one of the abandoned buildings in the West Bottoms, Miss?" he asked, turning his attention to Samantha.

"Yes."

"Could you find the place again?" Samantha thought she could. She'd seen signs on the fronts of a couple buildings and she remembered the tunnel. "I think so" she said, "if I can find any landmarks that I remember."

"If she can't, I think I can" I interjected.

"No" Samantha replied quickly, "you can't Sage." I must have looked at her with a "what the hell?" look on my face. He wasn't holding me in the same building where you found me," she said "but its not far from there... maybe two or three blocks."

Turning toward me Reynolds said, "Eight hours you say? How long has it been since you received the initial call?"

"About an hour and a half."

"Well Sage" Reynolds said, "I agree with your intuition. His hideout has worked well for him so far. Why change? Perhaps the little lady here can spot something familiar."

"Samantha" she said.

"Pardon?" Reynolds asked looking at her.

"My name is Samantha."

He regarded her in a curious manner. "Yes" he said, "Of course, Samantha. You may call me Blackie."

He stood an pulled his coat from the back of his chair. I hadn't realized it until he put it on, but it was a long, black duster like the James gang wore in the movie "The Long Riders" but black with a high collar and a short cape-like thing over the shoulders. We gulped the remainder of our beers and left the Empire Room.

"We'll take my rig." Reynolds said. "It's right over here." He pointed to a huge, black Ford pickup parked across the street. I noticed there was no chrome anywhere on the vehicle. Everything, even the bumpers, were black.

"I see you got a thing for black" I said. "I guess that's why they call you 'Blackie'."

"They call me Blackie" he said, "because my clothes are black, my hair is black, everything about me is black except for my asshole... and he's brown."

I laughed at that, but Samantha didn't seem to understand the joke. When I noticed she wasn't getting it, I said. "The guy that kidnapped you?" I said. "His name is Brown?"

Oh then she understood. "Brown... Asshole. Got it." she said. "It was kind of funny at that."

"Actually Samantha" Blackie said, "It's not so much my preference for one color over another as it is a necessity of the trade. You see my dear, in my business, stealth is everything."

We climbed in his huge truck, Samantha in the middle and me riding shotgun. "About your fee" I began, "I hate to ask but what do you charge?"

"I am never certain until the job is complete. It depends on the degree of danger, whether I am injured, that kind of thing. I can assure you, however, that it will not be inexpensive. I do not work 'pro bono', Mr. Chandler."

"I agree with your terms. Whatever it is, I'll be glad to pay it."

"Everyone is always happy to pay for my services" replied Reynolds.

We traveled at an easy pace. Samantha seemed happy about that because I guess I sometimes drive like I'm in a Nascar race, dodging in and out of traffic, speeding, ignoring yellow lights. She probably thinks I have a glove box full of traffic tickets.

Reynolds's driving was much more subdued than mine. Samantha could tell looking at me that it was driving me crazy. I wanted to get where we were going as fast as we could, especially since my children were in danger.

Suddenly Reynolds pulled into a grocery store parking lot and parked the truck. "Do you two have weapons?" he asked.

Samantha assured him that we were both well armed. Reynolds seemed uncomfortable with that idea.

"Can I assume you are both capable with your weapons?"

"Yes" I said, "I shoot pretty well. I have never seen Samantha shoot, but she took my Smitty apart pretty damn fast."

"I can shoot too" she said.

"Good" Reynolds said. "But we can't go charging into the West Bottoms like a heard of Bison. We need to formulate a plan."

After he had outlined his plan, Reynolds explained how we would enter the area and find the building where Sage had shot Max. "What was the name indicated on the front of the building?"

"Crane and Company" I replied.

"Alright, so we find the Crane building and park the truck. Then we try to retrace your footprints in reverse. Do you think you would recognize the building where you were being held, Samantha?"

She said she thought she would and Reynolds fired up the big truck and we were on the move again with me acting as navigator. I had a few direction problems for a while, which is understandable considering everything looks the same in this part of town: old and decrepit. After a few misdirections however, I successfully guided Reynolds to the Crane building. Before we got out of the truck, Reynolds made sure our guns were loaded and we had plenty of backup ammunition.

"Do not holster or in any way try to conceal your weapons" he said. "We may not have the luxury of surprise on our side. You don't want to be fumbling for your weapon in a rush."

We left the truck and walked toward the front door of the Crane building. "This is where it happed" I said. "This is where the bastard shot Papa."

"Is this the way you entered the building?" Reynolds asked Samantha indicating the front doors.

Samantha acknowledged the entrance.

"From which way did you come?"

"That way" she said pointing her finger.

"So you came from the south."

He began walking in the direction Samantha had pointed. She and I followed, Samantha first, then me. "I think you boys are protecting me by surrounding me." Samantha said.

After we'd walked a short distance, Reynolds stopped and turned to Samantha. "Do you recognize anything?'

She seemed surprised that she didn't really recognize anything. "Nothing looks familiar to me" she said. "It must have been the drugs. They must have fogged my memory." She said she felt like we were going the right way, but that the feeling was only intuition.

We walked a hundred yards or so farther in our linear formation before Reynolds stopped again to ask if anything looked familiar. We did that twice more before at last

Samantha saw what she called the tunnel. "I knew if I could find the tunnel, I'd have my bearings" she said.

"What tunnel?" I asked.

"There" she said pointing to a street.

"What is it?" Reynolds asked.

"The tunnel" she said, "See the tunnel? We walked down that tunnel on our way to the Crane building. There's an old paved street under it ridden with potholes."

"C'mon" she said, taking the lead.

We hurried to the tunnel and ducked under. Just as Samantha has said, the pavement was riddled with potholes.

"I guess no one drives here anymore" I said "so the city doesn't feel the need to keep the streets up."

"Indeed" said Reynolds. "It appears to have been abandoned and in disrepair for some time."

We walked up the tunnel toward some old buildings. Samantha remarked that the surroundings were looking very familiar to her.

"Up ahead and across the street" she said. "I think that's the building." As we hurriedly approached the building, I noticed some letters on the front of the building, but I couldn't string them together to make words. We walked on, randomly the letters appeared one by one. When we were just about to emerge from underneath the tunnel, I made out the name on the building: ""Kansas City Bolt, Nut, & Screw Co." The

Kansas City part was written in a script that resembled handwriting.

"That's the place" Samantha said.

"Are you certain?" asked Reynolds.

She assured him that I was. "I knew I had seen a name on the building, but I hadn't gotten the chance to look at it very long. I couldn't remember what it said until now. Seeing it again must have jogged my memory."

"Okay" I said. "So that's the place. What do we do now?"

"Well" Reynolds began, "now we wait and see if we can spot any movement or lights or any sign of anyone inhabiting the building."

We hunkered down behind a hedge that was growing across the street from the Kansas City Bolt & Nut building. It was strange, I thought, that the hedge was still there. The whole lot had almost gone back to nature. There were trees and shrubs growing all around what I assumed had been the front lawn of the brick building behind us. It was in shambles too. The roof had caved in some places allowing trees to grow through. The hedge itself had grown tall and ragged which made it a better place to hide.

I thought we should be doing something besides just waiting there behind that strange hedge, but Blackie said this was the best thing we could do right now. So we waited.

Chapter 23

Hughie was pacing the floor. He was the nervous type and it drove Max nuts. Max had never understood nervousness, or anxiety. Nothing much had ever really frightened him, and he'd never been close enough to anyone to care whether they lived or died. Having been estranged from his parents for almost 30 years probably hadn't helped the situation.

He'd heard terms bandied about by the shrinks he was forced to see as a child. "Sociopath" was usually what they dubbed him with. One asshole psychiatrist had referred to him as a future psychopath. "He'll probably become a serial killer" the good doctor had said. Those words had burned into Max's memory. He wasn't supposed to be listening, but that idiot doctor had left the door partially open while discussing his diagnosis with one of several pairs of Max's foster parents. He'd been placed in so many homes as a child, he'd lost count. He couldn't match any one of the numerous incidents of his life with any specific foster parents. They all kind of melded into one big bunch of losers.

He did remember one foster father that he'd kind of liked, and one that he hated with a passion. Those two stuck out in his memory Max had always figured because they were at opposite ends of the foster parent continuum. But Max had reset the lower limit of the continuum when he bashed that hateful foster father's head in with a rock when he was about 14 or 15.

The son of a bitch had taken Max fishing, just like his favorite foster father before him had done. He was beginning to think this guy might not be so bad, but once he got Max alone in the woods, he made sexual advances toward him. It was a big mistake. Max told the cops the man had tripped and fallen, hitting his head on a rock. Since there were no witnesses, or incriminating evidence pointing to his guilt, Max was simply sent to live with another foster family.

He didn't remember much about that family, but he did have one other memory of a time when he was smaller. He and a foster brother set fire to a shed beside someone's double-wide in a trailer park. The fire spread to the double-wide and burned the whole shebang to the ground. Max enjoyed that. He had no idea whose property he'd burned down, and it didn't matter anyway, but it was the biggest thrill of his life up to that point. He was probably around ten at the time, about the same age as little Jimmy.

No one had gotten hurt in the fire since no one was home at the time, which was partially the reason the fire department was delayed in arriving. It was the biggest rush he'd ever felt. The only thing that could have been better is if someone had been home and had died. He thought he'd been sent to another foster family after that, but couldn't remember for certain. Getting away with it was nice, but after feeling the rush of arson, Max knew he'd do it again even if he did get caught.

Max had never been afraid of anything. Even when they sent him to reform school, as they called child prison in those days, he was never afraid. He was always strong, stronger than guys four and five years his senior.

On his second night in reform school, four punks came to his room and attempted to kick his ass. They were surprised however when they found Max waiting for them. He'd been tipped off by another student that these four kids planned to beat hell out of him.

He confiscated a table knife from the cafeteria and a "Boy's Life" magazine from the library. He'd sharpened the table knife to a fine point by scraping it on the concrete floor that was beneath the carpet of his room. He rolled the magazine into a tight, baton-type weapon. When the four kids came into the room, Max was waiting for them behind the door. He'd propped some pillows in his bunk to make it look like he was in bed. He slept in the top bunk and had no roommate. Max wouldn't tolerate a roommate.

When the kids began beating on the pillows in the upper bunk, Max made his move. He struck first with his homemade baton. He thrust it into the lower back of one of the boys dropping him to his knees. He pulled out the knife and jammed into the kid's ear and twisted. The kid fell forward. Max didn't let go of the knife and it came out of the kid's ear as he fell to the floor.

He grabbed a second kid by his hair and shoved his face directly into the metal frame of the top bunk breaking his nose. He pulled the kid back by his hair exposing his throat. He hit the kid hard in the Adam's apple with the part of his hand between the thumb and forefinger sending the kid sprawling backward and falling into a heap on the floor.

Max set his sights on the two remaining kids on the other side of the bed. They looked scared to death. Max made a lunge for them but they dodged him. They made a mad dash for the door and were gone before Max could get to them.

He returned to check on the two he'd taken out. The kid who he'd knifed in the ear wasn't dead, but he wasn't in good shape either. The kid he had throat punched lay on the floor gasping for breath.

Max was thinking about finishing them both off just as three guards arrived and threw him against a wall. They spun him around and cuffed him. Two of the guards led him out of the room while the third stayed behind to inspect the damage.

The throat-punched kid was beginning to come around. He had finally stopped gasping, but blood was gushing from his broken nose. The other kid just lay on the floor, his eyes half shut, bleeding from the ear. There was some foamy substance coming out of his mouth. The guard suspected this kid was going to die. He radioed the school's paramedic team who arrived in less than a minute.

"He's been stabbed in the ear" a paramedic said. The guard found a bloody knife on the floor. "Probably with this" he said.

They took the kid to the infirmary and called for a doctor. The doctor called for an ambulance and the kid was taken to the hospital. There was little the doctors could do for the boy. Max's primitive lobotomy was irreversible.

The kid didn't die but he never returned to the reform school either. There was no need. Max's surgical procedure had not only permanently deafened the kid's right ear, but also removed all the wickedness from the boy; in fact, it pretty much removed his entire personality. The kid wasn't a vegetable exactly, but he was never capable of taking care of himself. He was unable to learn much of anything or become a functional member of society. He couldn't attend school or hold any kind of job. He lived with his parents until they became too old to care for him. Then he was placed in a retirement home where as far as Max knew, he still lived today.

Max had been hauled to "the hole" as it was referred to. It wasn't really a hole but a private, padded cell with no windows. He was kept there for a few days before he was hauled before a group of men who he did not know. The group expelled Max from the school. Not knowing what else to do with him, he found himself back in foster care again with new parents. Max was always proud of being the only kid he'd ever heard of who'd been expelled from reform school.

Suddenly Max was aware of Hughie's grating voice. "It's been over three hours since you made the call, Max" Hughie was saying. It brought Max back to the present reminding him of the pain his arm was causing him at the moment.

"I can tell time, Hughie" Max replied. "I don't need you acting like a fucking cuckoo clock every fifteen minutes."

Hughie returned to his pacing and viewing out the window. "I just thought we'd hear something by now" he said.

"Go check on the kids, Hughie. Make yourself useful."

Hughie left the room to go check on the Chandler children and their mother. They were locked up in the same dark room where Max had held Trixy.

"Are you folks alright?" Hughie asked entering the dark room. Everyone was seated on the same small mattress where Trixy had been only days before. The mother was on her knees. Both kids sat on their butts with their legs crossed Indian style.

"I need to go to the bathroom," Jimmy said.

"Well, go, then. Who's stopping you?"

"Where the hell do you want him to go, mister?" asked Kim. "He should just pee right here in this room?"

"Yes" answered Hughie. "This whole place is a shit hole. Nobody's gonna notice."   Hughie looked from person to person studying their faces and body language.

"How is everything else?" he asked. "Anyone need anything?"   The kids appeared satisfactorily frightened, but this woman was acting brazen again. Did she have heart or what?

Hughie approached and stood over her. "You gotta a problem with the boy pissing in the corner?"

"Yes I do asshole!"

Hughie backhanded her hard across the mouth splitting her lower lip causing it to bleed slightly.

"Don't mouth off to me, bitch!" he shouted. "I'll kill you just for entertainment and make your kids watch."

"Fuck you! What kind of vermin are you?"

Hughie backhanded her again, this time harder, almost knocking her over. "You don't learn too fast, do you bitch?" The kids were both screaming, almost hysterically.

"Shut up!" he screamed at them. The children's screams became whimpers. Hughie leaned close to Kim's ear. "I ain't vermin, lady. I used to be a computer programmer for a pretty big company."

It was true. Hughie had worked as a programmer for a good-sized software company that specialized in communications software, but the company was forced to sell to Gil Bates and his "Macroshit" company who laid off most of the company's programmers, Hughie among them. Hughie hadn't been able to find comparable employment since.

"No one's looking for field programmers anymore" he said. "Everyone just buys software off the shelf these days. So I may be a dinosaur, lady, but I ain't vermin." He stood over Kim breathing and trying not to come unglued.

"But I am desperate" he breathed. "So believe me when I tell you, you won't see the sunshine again if you mouth off to me one more time. He lowered his voice to a whisper. "And neither will these kids."

Hughie stood and walked back toward the door. "I guess everything is all right in here" he said. "I'll be back in an hour to check on you. Maybe I'll bring you some water."

Hughie closed the door and joined Max in the main room. "You should have told Chandler you'd kill that bitch wife of his first... leave those bastard kids motherless."

Max looked up at Hughie. I don't give a shit which one we kill first. They'll all be dead soon enough anyway." Max stood and looked out the window.

"So you are fixin' to kill 'em all?" Hughie asked after a few moments. Max turned and approached Hughie. "Damn right we're killing 'em" he said. "We ain't leaving any witnesses this time."

"I don't think I can kill children" Hughie said hesitantly.

A smile appeared on Max's face. "Oh sure you can" he said. "I'll tell you what. You can fuck the little girl before we kill her so she won't die a virgin if it makes you feel better."

Hughie turned suddenly. "What?" he stammered. "I, I'm not..."

"Oh Hughie. I'm doing you a favor. After tonight you won't be apprehensive about raping and shooting children anymore."

Was that supposed to be a joke? Hughie felt a sense of sickening righteousness inside him. "But they're just little kids, Max."

"Fuck 'em! They might be kids now, but they will grow up to be some high and mighty fuckers. Better we get rid of 'em now. Nip it in the bud."

"No" Hughie said as bravely as he could. "I will not be a party to raping and murdering children."

Max glared at him. Hughie braced himself for the inevitable punch but it never came.

"You'll be a party to whatever the fuck I say" Max said towering over Hughie. "I've never killed a kid either, Hughie, but I am not afraid to. What have you got against killing these little bastards?"

"It's not right, Max."

"None of what we are doing is right, Hughie. Do you think it's right to kidnap a mother and her two kids?"

"No, but I always thought we'd let them go after we got Chandler."

"We can't do that... We can't leave witnesses who've seen our faces."

Hughie felt ill. He couldn't believe that Max had intended to kill the whole family all along. He knew he would not get anywhere trying to convince him otherwise.

"If we get caught, Max" Hughie began, "we'll get sent back to prison forever. You know what they do to baby killers in prison?"

"I ain't going back to prison" Max said. "If they catch us, they're going to have to kill me cause I am not going back to prison... No way."

Hughie had always known Max was a sick fuck, but even he didn't think he'd kill children. Hughie couldn't bare that, and he certainly couldn't participate in murdering children. He went for a diversion.

"Maybe they won't call" he said. "Maybe Chandler's smarter than we thought."

"Yeah? And maybe he's already down there."   Max approached the window and glared out. He stood there a long while looking at everything, but seeing nothing.

"I want you to go down there and have a look around."

"What? Hughie exclaimed. "But Boss they might be down there already like you said. I might be walking into a trap."

"No. It's a good diversion. Chandler doesn't know you." Max turned from the window to face Hughie.

"Just go down there and act like you've got somewhere to go. Be nonchalant. Don't just stand there looking around like an idiot."

Hughie thought about the plan. At least it got him out of the building and away from Max.

"Nobody lives here except desperadoes, druggies and drunken bums" he said.

"Hey" Max exclaimed. "That's an even better idea. Go down there with a bottle of whiskey and just sit there looking like a homeless bum."

"I am a homeless bum" Hughie thought.

"We don't have any bottles of whiskey left" Hughie said.

Max glared at him and walked over close. He grabbed Hughie's shirt with his good hand and shook him. "Use your fucking head, Hughie" he said. "I don't want to hear anymore of your pissing and moaning... Got it?"

Hughie got it alright. He knew he'd have to figure out some way of getting himself out of this without getting killed. It probably meant prison, but even that would be better than hanging around Max. "Yes, sir" he said, "I got it. I'll do... something."

Hughie put his coat on and left. He wasn't sure what he was going to find outside or what he'd do once he got there, but he damn sure knew that Max would either beat the hell out of him, or shoot him if he disobeyed orders.

As Hughie exited the front door of the old warehouse, he stopped momentarily at the top of the steps and looked around. He saw nothing as was normal in this neighborhood at this time of night. He skipped down the stairs, turned left and began walking. He tried to act as though he had a destination, walking as deliberately as he could but still looking around in the bushes, and the shadows. He didn't really know what he was looking for. A person, a vehicle that wasn't normally there, or something out of place maybe.

Chapter 24

Driscoll and Marble were cruising the West Bottoms area but they saw nothing but wreckage and ruins. Suddenly a call came over the radio. It was dispatch reporting that the officers had entered the residence at 810 Grand Elm Street. There was no one home and nothing looked out of place until they looked in an upstairs bedroom which was a mess. The contents of a nightstand drawer was lying all over the floor, the bed was unmade, sheets and blankets on the floor. A damp towel lay on the floor as well. A desk was askew and a floor lamp tipped over. This was strange because the rest of the house appeared immaculate other than a half dozen empty beer cans in the living room.

"Sounds like something went on at the Chandler residence" Marble said.

"Yeah but what?" Driscoll said still looking at the now silent radio. "Sounds like evidence of a struggle."

"Do you think Mrs. Chandler had gone to bed?"

"Maybe but what did Max do? Rough her up in the bedroom and then have a few beers before leaving?"

"Doesn't make sense" Marble said. "Maybe he drank the beers first."

Driscoll looked at Marble. Was he kidding? Judging by the grin on his face she figured he must be kidding.

They continued cruising the West Bottoms area when suddenly Marble's cell phone rang. It was Jenkins. He apologized to Marble for the dispatcher's not releasing personal information. "Its procedure, Jack. You understand."

"Yes I do" Marble answered. "I wouldn't want Maxwell Brown to have access to my personal information."

"Right. Anyway, I don't have an address for the building you're looking for, but it must be in close proximity to the Crane building. The girl said the walk from where she was being held to the Crane building wasn't very far."

Marble thanked Jenkins for returning his call. "We're on our way."

Marble holstered his cell phone and looked over at Driscoll. "We were in the right vicinity at the Crane building." he said.

Chapter 25

"What luck" Blackie whispered. "He's coming out." Blackie, Samantha and I watched the man exit the front door of the Bolt and Nut building and stand on the front steps. He paused there to look around.

"That's not him" Samantha and I whispered in unison. We watched the man skip down the steps, turn left and begin walking down the street. He walked briskly.

"Know who he is?" Blackie asked. Samantha shook her head. "Never seen him before." she said. Blackie watched him intently.

"What are the chances that he's in this shitty neighborhood by accident?" he asked. Blackie figured that if he was not affiliated with Max, he probably had somewhere to go, probably a drug dealer's house or a crack house or something like that, maybe just to a bar. Otherwise he was just scouting.

"Sage" Blackie said, "Set your cell phone on vibrate." I did, and the he instructed me to follow the man down the street, but stay out of sight. "If he turns around" he said, "call my cell and let it ring only once. If he seems to be going somewhere else, call and let it ring twice. Got it?"

I assured him I did in fact have it and set off to follow the unidentified man. Samantha stayed with Blackie. Since she was an unknown commodity as far as her proficiency with her weapon was concerned, Blackie thought it best if she stayed with him.

I sneaked down the street behind the man, keeping my distance, yet keeping him in sight. He seemed to have a destination in mind. He walked briskly, not looking around much, not stopping. I stayed two blocks behind most of the time. I followed him for five blocks. I was just about to pull my cell phone and signal Blackie that he seemed to be going somewhere when suddenly, just before I pressed the send button, he stopped. He pulled out his cell phone, and made a call of his own. I could not hear any of the conversation from where I stood. After a very short call, the man turned and began walking toward me, the way he had come.

"Shit" I thought. I had to hide in a hurry or he would see me. I stayed close to the buildings. Luckily most of the streetlights were out so there was very little light. I found an inset doorway in an old brick building, and just backed into it and disappeared into the shadows.

I heard him approaching. I heard his shoes scuffing on the broken sidewalk. I held my breath and stood completely still. When he passed me, he glanced into the nook where I had concealed myself but he gave no sign of noticing me. I was very grateful when he walked briskly by without stopping. I was beginning to see the value in Blackie's concept of stealth.

I pulled out my cell phone and called the number Blackie had given me. It rang once and I hung up. I chanced a look. The man was a block away by now and moving fast. I waited until he was farther along before leaving the relative safety of my dark sanctuary.

Blackie's phone vibrated once. "He's on his way back" he said to Samantha. She and Blackie were still hiding in the bushes across the street from the Bolt and Nut building. It wasn't long before they spotted the man on his return trip. Blackie withdrew his Springfield .45 ACP and instructed Samantha to get her weapon ready, but to stay put. When the man was about 50 feet from the front door of the Nut & Bolt building, Blackie jumped out, pointed his gun at the man and shouted, "Hold it!"

The man stopped, looked at Blackie, and then looked at the door to the Nut & Bolt building. I could see he was evaluating his chances of making it if he ran. I was approaching him fast from behind. Blackie was closing in fast from his left. He must have decided he wouldn't make it to the door because he threw his hands in the air.

Blackie walked right up to him and stuck his Springfield right in his face. "I want to talk to you" he said. Blackie escorted him across the street and into the bushes where Samantha was waiting. Samantha checked him for weapons and sure enough, he was packing. He had a .38 revolver tucked in his belt in the back of his pants. When I finally got back, we walked the guy around the building behind us and down an alley. Blackie pressed him against the wall by pushing his Springfield into his ribs.

"Are you affiliated with Maxwell Brown" Blackie asked. The man didn't respond. He just stood there looking at Blackie with a stupid look on his face. So Blackie pushed the barrel of the Springfield into his ribs harder. The man winced but still didn't reply.

"Friend" Blackie said. "If you are not affiliated with Maxwell Brown, you have nothing to worry about. If you are, you might want to admit it now before some of your ribs begin to break."

It was awesome, like something from a Clint Eastwood movie. Here was Blackie shoving his pistol into this guy's rib which was obviously very painful. "Answer him for Christ's sake!" I said, but he just kept standing there silently.

Blackie handed me his pistol. Then he turned and threw a right into the guys face. The back of his head bounced off the side of the building and he was out cold. He went down face first, which didn't do his nose any favors.

As he lay bleeding, Blackie said, "Perhaps that will persuade him to be more verbose." He knelt down beside the man and rolled him onto his back. He lightly slapped his face a few times. "Come on, Boy" he said, "Wake up." After a few moments the guy came around. Blackie grabbed him by the front of his jacket and stood him up, back against the wall again.

"Would you like to tell us your name now?" he asked the man. The man glared at Blackie, then at me, then at Samantha. "You're her" he said absently. "You're that whore-" Blackie backhanded him before he could finish the sentence.

"Please refrain from calling people names" he said. "Now who are you?"

"Name's Hughie" he said. "Hughie Long."

"Ah" I thought, so this is the Hughie Long, Max's sidekick that Jenkins was talking about.

"Hughie, huh" replied Blackie. "Well alright, Hughie Long, are you in cahoots with Maxwell Brown?"

"He must be" Samantha said. "He obviously recognized me." She walked toward Hughie. "Were you a party to kidnapping me?" she asked.

"Yes, Ma'am" Hughie said. "I was." Now Samantha let him have it. She slapped him hard on the opposite side of his face from where Blackie had just backhanded him. His face reddened almost immediately.

"Damn you" she shouted.

"OK" Blackie said. "That's enough. So you are in bed with Maxwell Brown?" Hughie nodded.

Now I got into the act. I grabbed on to Hughie and threw him to the ground. I knelt down and put my knee in Hughie's chest.

"Are you holding my family up there?" I asked. Hughie tried to answer but couldn't seem to say anything. I just lost it. I began punching Hughie in the face repeatedly until Blackie pulled me off. I was so pissed off. Even Samantha said later she felt slightly sorry for Hughie. I managed to connect three or four times before Blackie stopped me.

"Whoa" Blackie said. "Sage, this will do no one any good." I stood over Hughie breathing heavily, seething in anger.

"Are you alright?" Blackie asked, helping Hughie to his feet and leaning him against the wall again. I wondered if Hughie felt as bad as he looked. I hoped so. His nose was bent to one side and bleeding, his eyes were beginning to swell; there was blood all over his face, dripping onto his shirt.

When Blackie was satisfied that Hughie was not hurt seriously, he said, "OK Hughie Long, we're going to need you to make a little phone call."

Hughie's eyes darted between Blackie and me. He seemed to be considering his situation. Finally he looked at Blackie and said, "Who do you want me to call?"

"Max" Blackie replied. "We want you to tell him you've got Sage and Samantha down here and you need help."

Hughie contemplated that for a second. "Why would I want to do that?"

"Because if you don't, you're going to jail for a long time for kidnapping" I said.

Hughie let his knees collapse underneath him and slid down the wall to a sitting position. "I ain't going down with him." he said.

"What?" I asked. "Who?"

"Max" Hughie answered. "I'm not taking the fall with him. He's crazy. I've been worried for a long time that he was going to kill me one day. He should be locked up forever." He let his head fall between his knees.

Blackie knelt down beside Hughie. "Then why don't you help us get him? You haven't really committed a crime yet, have you?"

He looked up at Blackie. "I helped him kidnap Chandler's family." I stepped forward and knelt down on the other side of Hughie.

"You did that under duress, Hughie. You were afraid for your own life. You were afraid that if you didn't go along with Max, he'd kill you." Hughie looked a little more relieved.

"Do you think a jury would believe that?"

"Oh sure" I said. "Happens all the time." Hughie became silent again. He thought about the offer for a few minutes without saying a word. Finally he said, "If I help you guys, we gotta get him. He will kill me if I betray him by siding with you boys and then we fuck it up."

"We won't fuck it up" Blackie said. "Get on your cell phone and call Max. Get him out here. Tell him you have Sage and Samantha captured but you need assistance."

"Trixy" I said.

"What?" asked Blackie turning to look at me.

"Trixy" I repeated. "Max knows Samantha as Trixy."

Blackie nodded in agreement. "Alright then" he said. "Tell him you have captured Sage and Trixy and you need help getting them upstairs."

Chapter 26

Max was becoming impatient. Where the hell was Hughie? If that little fucker ran off and left him here, he'd be one sorry little computer geek. He paced the floor. He couldn't see anything but a side street from his vantage point and there was nothing happening there. Hughie had been gone for over thirty minutes. Where was he? Did they get him? Ah shit, he thought.

He went to check on the hostages. He opened the door and everyone was still sitting on the old mattress. "Everyone OK in here?" he asked.

"I really need to go to the bathroom" Jimmy answered.

"Fine" Max said calmly. He reached down and grabbed Jimmy by the back of his shirt and picked him up. He hauled him to a corner in the room. "Go ahead and piss, Jimmy" he commanded.

Jimmy did. He was in bad shape by now. If he didn't pee now, he'd probably not make it to a bathroom. When he finished, Max said, "Good boy. Now zip up your pants and let's go join your mother and sister."

Max left the room without saying anything further. After another five minutes of pacing and trying to see something through the window, Max was about to lose it. He was convinced that Hughie had left. Now his only choice would be to shoot the hostages and get out of there. If there was anyone downstairs, he'd shoot them too on his way out. Then he'd find that fucking Hughie and dust his ass just on general principles. Max had just about made up his mind that his new plan was the way to go when his cell phone rang.

"Where the hell are you?" he growled into the phone. Hughie was telling him something that was making him smile. He had somehow sneaked up on Chandler, and that whore, Trixy. Why was she still with him?

Hughie had them tied up outside across the street in some bushes. Max put his face as close to the window as possible and tried to see the bushes across the street, but he wasn't in the right position. He left the room and walked across the hall to a room that looked out on the street where Hughie was.

"Holy shit!" Max exclaimed. Sure enough, there was Hughie standing above some bushes. Chandler and the whore were lying on the ground with their hands tied behind their backs.

"God damn" Hughie, Max said. "I didn't think you had it in you to do that kind of work." Max continued viewing out the window at the scene below. He was smiling like a hungry man looking at a feast.

"Shoot 'em!" he said. "Shoot 'em both in the head, Hughie."

Chapter 27

Hughie was standing over Samantha and me. We were doing our best to portray the part of captives. Blackie was hiding a few feet away with his pistol trained on Hughie in case he tried anything.

"I thought you'd want to do that, Max" said Hughie. "I've never killed anyone, and I really don't want to start now." Hughie actually had no weapon, but he was doing his best to hide that fact from Max. He was speaking very softly and very calmly to Max, trying to persuade him to come out and shoot Trixy and me.

"You said you wanted to shoot this fucker in the arm so he'd know what it felt like." Hughie was silent for a few seconds, then "Yeah... yeah, OK, hurry." When Hughie snapped his cell phone shut, I knew Max must be on his way.

"What am I going to do?" asked Hughie. "When Max gets here, he's going to expect me to help him." He checked the door to the building to see if Max was coming out. "Give me my gun back" he said to Blackie.

Blackie didn't think that was the best idea he'd heard all day. Hughie was obviously rattled. "But I need something!" he said.

"You'll be fine, Hughie" Blackie assured him.

Suddenly Max appeared outside the building. He came very quickly across the street. Samantha and I were supposed to remain in position until Blackie made his move. When Max stepped up on the broken sidewalk, Blackie jumped up. "Stop right there" he said. Max stopped, looking very surprised. Samantha and I jumped to our feet, weapons pulled. All in all there were three guns trained on Max.

"What the hell is this shit, Hughie?" he asked. Hughie didn't reply. Instead Blackie said, "You're done, Max. We're holding you here until the police arrive... Sage? Call the police and then go get your family."

I didn't hear that last part. "What?" I asked. Blackie turned his head from Max to me and repeated what he had just said. It wasn't long, but it was just enough time for Max to suddenly leap behind the bushes. Blackie couldn't see him from where he was, but obviously Max could see us.

A shot rang out from behind the bushes and Hughie went down. Blackie hit the dirt and lay flat. His black clothing made him almost invisible. Samantha and I scattered in different directions. I ran behind a large, oak tree and Samantha bolted around the corner of the building behind us. Although Max couldn't see us clearly, he was shooting in our general direction. One of the bullets came so close, I heard it whiz by like a high speed bumblebee on steroids.

Driscoll and Marble heard the shots. They had been staying pretty close to the Crane building until they got a better lead.

"Holy shit!" exclaimed Marble. "Where did those shots come from?"

"Over there, I think" exclaimed Driscoll pointing out the passenger side car window. Marble took a right at the next street and floored it. They drove high speed down the dark street hoping there would be no pedestrians. More shots rang out; closer this time.

Hughie was on the ground. He was gurgling and spitting and trying to talk. I figured he was saying he'd been hit; that Max had shot him, but I wasn't. He sounded bad. I figured he was dying and there was nothing anyone could do for him.

Max was moving farther away, I fired blindly into the bushes but hit nothing but twigs. Suddenly Max stood and ran behind a large tree. He had somehow moved a good half block away. How the hell did he do that?

Samantha took a shot at the tree to try to get Max on the move again, but it didn't work. Blackie had made his way closer to the bushes, and was kneeling trying to see where Max had been hiding.

"He's behind that big tree" I said. Blackie suddenly got to his feet but remained low. He ran down the hedge toward the tree where Max was hiding. Max fired a few shots but none of them found their mark. Samantha and I shot back to give Blackie some cover fire. We managed to keep Max sequestered behind the tree, but he must have realized what was happening because he suddenly charged from behind the tree staying low but moving very fast toward the Bolt and Nut building's front entrance. He was running in a zigzag pattern.

We all opened fire. Blackie was shooting over the hedge. Samantha was using the corner of the building to steady herself and blazed away. I stepped from behind my tree and began firing, but I couldn't hit him. None of us could. Every time I thought I had a good shot, he would zigzag again and I'd lose him in the darkness. Miraculously, Max wasn't hit. He made his way to the door and entered the building.

"Shit!" I said. Blackie came back to check on Hughie. It was too late. He was gone. Without any further delay, Blackie shouted, "Let's go before he has time to get in position."

We ran as fast as we could across the street to the Nut and Bolt building. We were all snuggled up as close to the wall as we could get so Max couldn't see us if he was looking down. Blackie made a motion with his head. I understood. We both rolled out from our hiding places and charged the door, pistols before us. There was no one at the door, which was a big relief, until I realized that mean he must be upstairs with Kim and the kids again. Damn it!

Blackie opened the door and raced in. I followed him and Samantha followed me. There was a stairway to the left and a hallway to the right. "Go that way" Blackie said, indicating the hallway between the two staircases, "in case he went that way." He turned and ascended the stairs.

"Stay here" I told Samantha. "If Max comes down those stairs, shoot him." I turned and headed down the hallway as far as it went. There was no one there and there were no back stairs. I returned almost immediately.

"Okay" I said to Samantha. "I'm going up." Unsure what to do, Samantha followed me. We reached the top without running into Max which half surprised me. The staircase opened to a huge vestibule area with four hallways, one going in each direction.

"Damn!" I whispered. "Which way do you think Blackie went?" Samantha didn't speak; she just shook her head and shrugged her shoulders. We stood listening intently trying to hear something that would indicate which way we should go. Suddenly from the hallway to our right, there was a gunshot. We scrambled down the hall as fast as we could. Halfway down the hall, we saw Blackie. He was down. I thought he'd been hit by the gunshot.

"Get down" he whispered when he saw us approaching. We dropped to the floor.

"He's in there" Blackie said pointing to a closed door a bit further down the hall and to the left.

"Who shot?" I whispered.

"Max shot at me through the door, but he missed." We all lay sprawled on the floor. I was pretty nervous wondering what Blackie planed to do. I felt like a sitting duck there on the floor. Blackie looked at me and made a motion with his head that I took to mean retreat, so staying low we ran back down the hallway to the vestibule.

"What are we going to do?" I asked.

"This is a bad one, alright" Blackie said. "I am not certain at this point what we should do." He stroked his beard. He was obviously trying to come up with a plan.

Marble and Driscoll followed the sounds of the gunshots down the street. Suddenly Driscoll yelled "There it is!"

"Where?"

"Right there. See?"

Marble looked slightly to his right. Sure enough in big block letters, "Kansas City NUT & BOLT CO." He whipped the car to the curb, Driscoll bailing out before Marble could stop completely. She ran to the front doors and waited for Marble and the other officers to catch up. She was going in first this time damn it.

Blackie had been studying on a plan for the last few minutes. I was afraid he wasn't going to come up with anything. Suddenly he said "Call him."

"What?"

"Call Max's cell phone and try to keep him talking." Not knowing what else to do, I took out my cell phone and looked up Papa's number and hit send. I wasn't sure he still had Papa's phone, or that he would answer if he did.

"Yeah?" he said when he answered the phone. I didn't know exactly what Blackie had in mind or what I should say to a madman to keep him on the phone. I figured stroking his ego couldn't hurt. "You're good" I said. "You got away from us and we had three guns. I'm impressed."

"Fuck you" he said. "You're family is dead." My heart sank. I felt a panic like never before.

"If" he added, "you don't get outta here right now."

"It's me you want, Max, not my family. Let's trade."

Blackie was sneaking down the hallway trying to get close to the door. I began talking a bit louder so Blackie would be able to hear me.

"Just let my kids go. They've done nothing to you or anyone else."

"Nah" he said. "I'd lose my advantage if I did that. You probably don't give a shit about your ex-wife... I wouldn't." He was right. Well not completely right, but at that moment I would have sacrificed Kim for the safety of the kids in a heartbeat. It wasn't so much that I didn't care about Kim, but the kids were the priority.

"Well then, what do you want to do, Max?"

"I'm not sure yet, but if you push me, the boy dies first."

Blackie had made his way down the hall, past the door. He was silently checking the door on the other side. Luckily, it was open. He went in. I could see the logic of his plan now. Perhaps there was an adjoining door between the office he entered and where Max and the kids were, or if I could coax Max outside, Blackie could strike from behind.

I remained silent for a while. I was giving Max some time to work things out.

"You still there?" Max asked.

"Yes, I am."

"You're in a bad way, Chandler" he said. "I'm holding all the cards. You got shit."

Driscoll, Marble and the two other officers had entered the building, but they had no idea which way to go. There were stairs on either side of a wide hallway. Marble directed the two officers to follow the hallway.

"Do you think they would be upstairs or down?" Marble asked.

"Hell if I know" answered Driscoll. "Should we check both?"

"Better stay in pairs... Safer that way."

They decided to ascend the staircase and see where that led them.

Max was right about me holding no cards, and I knew it, but I wasn't sure I wanted to confirm it just yet. I was thinking that if Max suspected I had some kind of ace in the hole, it might keep him off guard a little. I didn't want him overly-confident that he could kill us all and walk away from this.

"Hughie is dead" I said unable to think of anything better to say at the moment.

"Good" he said. "That turncoat son of a bitch deserves to be dead."

"So you have the whole fifty thousand to yourself, Max. You don't have to share it with anyone. Just leave now, go somewhere, Mexico maybe." I was hoping he'd take the bait and believe I'd let him walk out of there. I wasn't really lying. Oh I wanted to see him dead for what he put Samantha and my kids through, but I'd let him walk. He could have the money free and clear. My concern was the safe return of my kids... and Kim too, it that was possible.

"My kids are all that matter to me, Max. Just take the money and run. We won't try to stop you or call the cops."

Max thought that might be his best bet, but he wasn't sure I meant it. I tried harder to convince him that I was telling the truth. All I wanted was the safe return of my children. I'm sure he believed that, but he just wasn't sure enough to just walk out the door.

I decided to sweeten the deal. "I'll even give you another fifty thousand if you just leave now" I offered.

"You don't have fifty grand on you right now, do you?" he asked. "So what are you gonna do, send it to me? No way Chandler, I'm holding all the cards here. We're doing this my way."

I agreed. He did have the upper hand at the moment. "Okay" I said. "What is your plan then?"

"I'm coming out, but I'm bringing your son with me. So get ready." My phone lost connection. He'd hung up on me. Damn it! I was supposed to keep him on the phone as long as I could. Suddenly, the door popped open, and I saw Jimmy coming out the door with a huge arm around his waist. I noticed his feet weren't touching the floor.

Max emerged from the doorway and looked down the hall at me. "Drop your weapon" he said, "and kick it down here to me."

I gently laid my Smith on the floor, kicked it down the hallway. It made a scuffling sound as it slid along the floor. I stood with my hands in the air. I'd never felt so terribly vulnerable in all my life. "Okay, Max, my weapon is on the floor. Take it easy."

"Where are your friends?"

Driscoll and Marble had cautiously ascended the stairs. They now stood in the vestibule with the other two officers who had returned saying the hallway went nowhere but to the other side of the building. There were some offices to the right and left, but the doors were all locked. There had been no sigh on anyone entering them.

"Which way?" Marble asked. "Which way would they go?"

Marble instructed the officers to move forward and check out the hallways ahead of them. "Be careful" he said, "This guy is armed and dangerous."

The two officers walked slowly ahead, guns drawn and held in front of them.

"Listen." Driscoll said. "I think I hear voices."

"I chanced a glance at Samantha and mouthed the words "stay there." I looked back at Max and said, "Blackie is right here beside me. I told the girl to stay downstairs."

"Blackie?" Max asked. "Who the hell is Blackie?"

As if on cue, Blackie stepped out from his hiding place behind Max. "I am" he said. Max turned to face Blackie. I motioned for Samantha to step out into the hallway. Max fired. Blackie went down. Max turned around to face me and Samantha fired. The bullet hit Max right between the eyes. He let go of Jimmy.

"Get outta there, Jimmy!" I yelled. Jimmy bolted back inside the door.

Suddenly from behind I heard a voice. "Hold it!" Samantha disregarded the voice and fired again this time catching Max in the chest. He stumbled backward, fired his gun once, but it was pointing at the floor. Suddenly he collapsed to his knees and slowly fell forward. I ran toward him and stripped his weapon from his hand. He didn't move. I rolled him over and felt for a pulse. There was none. Max was dead.

I turned to find people behind us with their guns trained on us. "Police! Drop your weapon" one said.

"I have no weapon" I said putting my hands in the air.

Samantha had run to Blackie who was still down and not moving.

"Drop your weapon!" the voice said again, this time louder. I suddenly realized he was talking to Samantha.

"Drop you weapon, Samantha!" I yelled.

She put the gun on the floor but didn't raise her hands. Instead she knelt down and felt Blackie's throat for a pulse and found one. "He's not dead" she yelled back, "but he's not moving either."

The four people approached. Two were uniformed officers, another wore plain clothes and the fourth was wearing a Department of Corrections jacket, a Parole Officer's jacket.

"Get on the floor!" yelled the plainclothesman.

I did and looked over at Samantha who was already on the floor. Not on her belly, but still kneeling beside Blackie. She didn't take instruction very well I thought.

Suddenly Blackie started to move. "God damn, that hurt" he said struggling to sit up.

"Stay down, sir" said the man in the plainclothes who by now was standing over me.

"Is he dead?" Blackie asked indicating Max's body. I assured him that he was. Blackie unbuttoned his shirt and I saw the reason he was still alive. Max hadn't missed. Blackie's bullet-proof vest had saved him. He opened the vest and I could see a huge red spot on the left side of his chest.

"That's gonna leave a hell of a bruise" Samantha said.

"Yeah" Blackie said, "that's gonna cost ya, Sage."

Driscoll and Marble had by now figured out who we were, and confirmed that Max was truly dead.

"What happened here?" Marble asked.

"He was holding my family hostage in that room" I answered. "If you will allow me to get up, we can go see if they are all right."

Marble nodded.

I stood and ran into the room and found the kids were unharmed. Jimmy had already untied Lisa, and was busy freeing Kim. When she saw me, Lisa came running over and hugged me. Then Jimmy hugged me and Kim stepped up to where Jimmy and I stood, her face badly bruised, one eye swollen shut.

"Thank you, Sage" she said. "I thought we were goners." We reunited for a while longer. Samantha and Blackie stepped into the room.

"I couldn't have done it without these two" I said. "Everyone, this is Blackie Reynolds and Samantha Johnson. Blackie, Samantha, this is my ex-wife, Kim and my children, Lisa and Jimmy."

Kim and the kids all thanked Blackie and Samantha and shook hands all around.   "Blackie Reynolds" Marble said as he approached with his right hand extended.   "It is a pleasure. You know, you're something of a legend at the Western Division."

Blackie shook hands with the man. "And you are?"

"Detective Jack Marble, Western Division."

"I've heard the name. Very nice to meet you too."

Marble introduced himself and Officer Driscoll to everyone. Driscoll shook hands all around.

"So do we have a crime here?" Blackie asked.

"What do you think?" Marble asked Driscoll.

"I think what we have is a textbook case of self-defense."

"No" I interjected. "There was a crime here."   Everyone turned to look at me with question-marked faces.

"Outside across the street" I said. "You will find the body of Max's accomplice. Max shot him."

I walked over to Samantha and hugged her. "You weren't kidding" I whispered. "You are one hell of a shot."

"Told you so" she whispered back. I pulled back a little and kissed her long and hard. I knew Kim would be staring at us, probably the kids too, but I didn't care. I was in love.

Epilogue

We had plenty of witnesses to corroborate our story, including three police officers and a member of the Department of Probation and Parole. No charges were filed. Marble and Driscoll were actually relieved Max was dead. Now Driscoll didn't have to worry about giving him enough rope to hang himself. The authorities weren't real happy that we'd taken the law into our own hands, but they understood that we really had no other choice. Besides, Blackie was a legend with law enforcement officials. No one was willing to blow his cover by dragging him into court for the murder of a piece of shit like Maxwell Brown.

Poor Hughie. We hadn't meant for him to die. We all felt bad about that, but there wasn't really anything we could have done differently.

A few weeks later, everything was back to normal. Samantha and I moved into a better place, a little two bedroom house we found not far from my old place, but it was a lot nicer. The seller wanted out from under it, so I bought it for a good price.

Samantha fixed the place up nice. We setup housekeeping. I have never been so happy in my life. We go to the shooting range once in a while. Samantha out shoots me every time.

With help from a therapist, Kim and the kids were getting past their trauma. Spring was on the way and Jimmy was planning to play little league for the first time. I volunteered as assistant coach and we practiced every weekend. The kids really liked Samantha. They stay at our house now and then and we watch movies and eat popcorn. It's almost like having my family back.

I got the bill from Blackie. He was right; it was high, but actually not as high as I thought it might be. Plus, he was worth every penny. He'd charged me extra for his being shot just like he said he would. Even though he'd worn the vest, the bullet had fractured two ribs.

Samantha and I returned to the Empire Room to see Blackie once. He wasn't there but we stayed a while anyway. We had a couple of beers and listened to the pianos. I remembered what Blackie had said about music: that it's the art of the truly enlightened. Sitting there listening to the pianos do battle in harmony, I thought he might just be on to something there. Maybe I should learn something about music. It is one of the things that make life worth living. It's a uniquely human experience. Even though I haven't seen him since that night at the Nut and Bolt Factory, I think a lot about Blackie and am thankful for his being there when I needed him.

THE END

Made in the USA
Charleston, SC
20 December 2009